THE MIDNIGHT WHISTLE: 50 EPIC BEDTIME STORIES FROM THE WORLD OF SOCCER

A BRIEF HISTORY OF THE BEAUTIFUL GAME

SAM CRESTWELL

CONTENTS

Before We Begin vii
Kick Off ix

1. The Magic of First Touches: A Brief History Of Soccer — 1
2. Night of Underdogs: Leicester City's Premier League Triumph — 4
3. Dreams in Sky Blue: Manchester City's Rise — 7
4. The Miracle of Istanbul: Liverpool's 2005 Champions League Victory — 10
5. Socceroos' Leap of Faith: Australia's 2006 World Cup Journey — 13
6. Zidane's Headbutt: A Moment of Madness — 16
7. The Fall and Rise of AC Milan — 19
8. Ajax's Youth Revolution: Breeding Ground of Legends — 23
9. The Senegal Lions' Roar: 2002 World Cup Odyssey — 27
10. Mohamed Salah: Egyptian King — 30
11. The Italian Stallion: Francesco Totti's Roma Love Affair — 32
12. Didier Drogba: Uniting a Nation Through Football — 35
13. Sunil Chhetri: The Indian Football Dream — 38
14. The Resilience of Chapecoense — 40
15. The Golden Generation: Belgium's Rise — 43
16. The Danish Dynamite: Denmark's 1992 European Triumph — 46
17. Japan's Women Warriors: 2011 World Cup Victory — 49
18. The Humble King: Kaka's Journey of Faith — 52
19. The American Dream: Clint Dempsey's Trail from Texas — 55
20. The Phoenix: Landon Donovan's Comeback — 58

21. The Tactical Maestros of Italy — 61
22. Germany's Rebirth: The 2014 World Cup Strategy — 64
23. The Dutch Total Football Legacy — 67
24. France's Multicultural Triumph: 1998 and 2018 World Cups — 70
25. The Evolution of Goalkeeping — 73
26. The South American Flair: Dribbling Through History — 76
27. Spain's Tiki-Taka: Dominance Through Possession — 79
28. The Celtic Tigers: Ireland's 1990 World Cup Journey — 82
29. The Rise of Football Academies: La Masia and Beyond — 85
30. The Psychology of Penalty Shootouts — 88
31. Technology in Football: VAR and Beyond — 91
32. The Unseen Heroes: Football Scouts — 94
33. The Miracle of Bern: Germany's 1954 World Cup — 97
34. The Passion of Buenos Aires: Boca Juniors vs. River Plate — 100
35. The Green Brigade: Celtic's Vocal Support — 103
36. The Yellow Wall: Borussia Dortmund's 12th Man — 106
37. The Ibrox Disaster: Tragedy and Triumph of Human Spirit — 109
38. The Tragedy and Triumph of Hillsborough — 112
39. The Class of '92: Manchester United's Golden Generation — 117
40. The Galácticos: Real Madrid's Stars of the Early 2000s — 120
41. The Sound of Silence: Playing Behind Closed Doors — 123
42. Football in Warzones: The Power of Sport — 126
43. One-Armed Striker: Scoring Against Odds — 129
44. Bright Lights - Youngest Footballer in the UK — 132
45. The Heartbeat of Paris: A Tale of a Footballing City — 135

46. Losing Points Off The Field: Controversial
    Points Deduction   138
47. The Day the VP Strapped On His Boots   142
48. A Tale Of Patience: 19 Years Between Two
    Games   145
49. The Most Brutal Game In History   148
50. The Little Giants: San Marino's Journey of
    Hope and Heart   151
    Conclusion   154

BEFORE WE BEGIN

You will find that we interchangeably use the word "football" to describe soccer. A different word for the same beautiful sport that unites us all.

KICK OFF

Under the shimmering floodlights, a football match unfolds—a spectacle of passion, skill, and the collective heartbeat of fans around the globe. There's nothing quite like the electric atmosphere of a stadium brimming with anticipation, where every cheer, gasp, and chant encapsulates the universal thrill that football brings to its faithful followers. It's in these moments, amidst the fervent roars and the suspense of the next goal, that the true spirit of the game comes alive, weaving together stories of triumph, despair, resilience, and unity.

My journey with football has been a lifelong affair, marked by the joy of attending five World Cups and the privilege of coaching youth soccer in the United States. From the terraces to the touchline, my love for the game has taken me from being a fan to becoming a storyteller, chronicling the rich history of football's most unforgettable moments. As a best-selling author and a seasoned football historian, I've had the honor of bringing the magic of the game to readers worldwide, sharing tales that resonate with the heart and stir the soul.

In "The Midnight Whistle: 50 Epic Bedtime Tales from the World of Soccer," I aim to take you on a global journey through football's most epic tales, stories that captivate, engage, inspire, and educate. Unlike the usual fare of statistics, player biographies, or technical breakdowns, this book celebrates the magical, often overlooked moments that define the beautiful game. From underdog victories and legendary comebacks to personal feats of resilience and triumph, these tales are a testament to the indomitable spirit of football and those who live and breathe it.

This book is for you, the adult football fan who seeks more than just the game. It's for those who find inspiration in the grit and grace of players on and off the pitch, who see football as a mirror reflecting the highs and lows of life itself. As you delve into these tales, I encourage you to reflect on their meanings, jot down your thoughts, or consider how each story mirrors your own experiences. This interactive journey is not just about reading; it's about connecting, learning, and finding inspiration in the universal language of football.

So, I invite you to join me on this voyage through the heart and soul of football. Let's explore these tales together, with an open heart and a curious mind, and discover the power of football to inspire dreams, ignite passion, and change lives. Welcome to "The Midnight Whistle," where every story is a kickoff to a dream.

Let the journey begin.

1

THE MAGIC OF FIRST TOUCHES: A BRIEF HISTORY OF SOCCER

In the realm of global sports, few phenomena can claim the pervasive, enduring allure that football holds. This game, a simple pursuit involving a ball and two goals, transcends geographical boundaries, socioeconomic divides, and cultural differences, knitting a history of shared humanity across the planet. It's a sport where the act of a child kicking a makeshift ball in a dusty alley resonates with the precision of a professional player in a stadium filled with tens of thousands.

Football, in its essence, is more than just a game; it's a universal language spoken fluently by millions worldwide, irrespective of their native tongue. The fervor it ignites is not confined to the parameters of a pitch; it spills over into homes, cafes, and streets, fostering a sense of community and belonging among strangers.

Tracing the lineage of football leads us to ancient civilizations where similar ball games were played as part of religious ceremonies or communal festivities. From the Han Dynasty's cuju to the Indigenous peoples of Mesoamerica's ulama, these early forms of the game bear witness to humanity's longstanding fascination with ball games. However, the football we recognize today started taking shape in England during the 19th century, where it evolved from a chaotic and unregulated village activity into a structured sport with codified rules.

This transformation was not merely about organizing chaos into order; it marked the beginning of football's journey from local fields to global stadiums. The establishment of The Football Association in 1863 laid down the foundational rules, giving rise to a sport that would captivate hearts and minds worldwide.

The impact of football on society is profound and multi-faceted, acting as both a mirror and a molder of social dynamics. In times of political upheaval or social unrest, football has offered a semblance of normalcy and a temporary escape for people. For instance, during World War I, the Christmas Truce of 1914 saw opposing soldiers in the trenches momentarily set aside their weapons to play football, highlighting the sport's power to bridge insurmountable divides.

Moreover, football clubs often become symbols of local identities and pride, reflecting the social, economic, and historical nuances of their communities. The loyalty fans feel towards their teams is akin to familial bonds, passed down through generations, creating a legacy of shared memories and experiences.

The universal appeal of football lies in its ability to unite people from vastly different backgrounds. A striking example of this unity can be observed during international tournaments like the FIFA World Cup, where fans from around the globe converge, draped in their national colors, yet bonded by their mutual love for the game.

This shared passion often leads to spontaneous acts of camaraderie among fans, transcending linguistic and cultural barriers. A conversation between a Brazilian and a German, with no common language but football, can lead to an exchange of stories, laughter, and perhaps, lifelong friendship. Such moments underscore football's role as a unifying force, capable of fostering global solidarity.

As much as football is about unity, it is also the genesis of some of the most intense rivalries known to the sports world. These rivalries, often rooted in historical, cultural, or political differences, add a layer of depth and excitement to the game. The El Clásico, a term that conjures images of fierce battles between Real Madrid and FC Barcelona, is not just about football; it's a reflection of the historical and cultural rivalry between Castile and Catalonia.

These matches are not merely about the ninety minutes on the clock; they are about honor, pride, and sometimes, centuries-old legacies. The anticipation and emotions surrounding such games elevate them from mere sporting events to cultural phenomena, witnessed by millions around the world.

In sum, football's journey from ancient ball games to the modern spectacle enjoyed by billions is a testament to its enduring appeal and profound impact on the human experience. It's a sport that continues to write its history, one goal, one match, and one fan at a time, weaving an ever-expanding story of passion, unity, rivalry, and above all, love for the game.

Let dive straight into some of the greatest stories to have come from The Beautiful Game.

2

NIGHT OF UNDERDOGS: LEICESTER CITY'S PREMIER LEAGUE TRIUMPH

In terms of feel-good football tales, few stories are as vibrant and heartwarming as the story of Leicester City in the 2015-2016 Premier League season. Before the start of the season, Leicester, a team that had barely avoided relegation the previous year, was considered a long shot for the title, with odds of 5000-1 against them. What unfolded over the next nine months was a tale of determination, strategy, and unity, that not only defied those odds but also rewrote the script of what's possible in football.

At the heart of Leicester City's success was a simple yet profound belief in the impossible. The team, led by the unassuming Claudio Ranieri, embarked on the season with modest expectations from the outside world. However, within the club's walls, there was a growing sense of belief. Each match, whether against a team at the top of the table or one fighting relegation, was approached with the same intensity and commitment. This unwavering focus turned potential into points, as

Leicester started to climb the table, transforming from underdogs to title contenders.

Claudio Ranieri, affectionately known as 'The Tinkerman' from his previous managerial stints, showcased a masterclass in tactical flexibility and innovation throughout the season. Contrary to his nickname, Ranieri adopted a consistent approach at Leicester, utilizing a 4-4-2 formation that leveraged the team's strengths and neutralized their opponents. The tactical cornerstone of Leicester's play was a compact, disciplined defense coupled with fast, counter-attacking football. This approach turned Jamie Vardy and Riyad Mahrez into household names, as they terrorized defenses with their pace and skill. Ranieri's ability to instill a tactical system that maximized his squad's potential while fostering a strong defensive unit was pivotal in their title-winning campaign.

In an era where football is often dominated by teams boasting star-studded lineups, Leicester City's triumph was a refreshing reminder of the power of teamwork. The squad was a cohesive unit, with every player understanding their role and contributing to the team's success. The midfield dynamism of N'Golo Kanté, the defensive solidity of Wes Morgan and Robert Huth, and the creative flair of Mahrez all played their part. Yet, it was the collective effort, the willingness to fight for each other, and the shared belief in their cause that set Leicester apart. This emphasis on team spirit over individual brilliance underscored the importance of unity, showcasing how a group of committed individuals could achieve greatness together.

Leicester City winning the Premier League did more than just etch their names into football history; it ignited a flame of hope among smaller clubs around the world. The message was clear: with the right mix of belief, strategy, and teamwork, the seemingly impossible could be achieved. Clubs with modest budgets and resources saw in Leicester a blueprint for success, challenging the notion that financial power alone dictates footballing achievements. This legacy of hope continues to inspire teams facing daunting odds, reminding them that on the football pitch, dreams can, and do, come true.

In the end, Leicester City's story is not just about a football club winning a title; it's a story that resonates with anyone who believes in the power of dreams. It's a testament to the unpredictable, magical nature of football, where determination, strategy, and unity can overturn even the most improbable odds.

3

DREAMS IN SKY BLUE: MANCHESTER CITY'S RISE

The story of Manchester City's ascent from the depths of English football's lower leagues to the pinnacle of the Premier League is a tale that captures the imagination. It's a journey of transformation, fueled by ambition, strategic foresight, and an unwavering commitment to playing beautiful football. Once overshadowed by their illustrious neighbors, Manchester United, City's journey to becoming one of the game's elite is a testament to the power of vision and investment.

For decades, Manchester City oscillated between moments of brilliance and periods of struggle, often finding themselves in the shadow of Manchester United's global success. The turn of the millennium saw City grappling with the challenges of lower league football, a far cry from the glittering stages they aspired to grace. However, the club's fortunes took a dramatic turn in 2008 with the acquisition by the Abu Dhabi United Group. This marked the beginning of a new era, not just in terms of financial muscle, but in the ambition and vision for what Manchester City could become. The transformation was gradual but determined, as City began to climb the ranks, both domestically and on the European stage.

The metamorphosis of Manchester City into a powerhouse was underpinned by strategic investments that went beyond merely acquiring top-tier talent. Yes, the influx of world-class players was a significant part of the strategy, but the vision was more holistic. The club invested in state-of-the-art training facilities, the Manchester City Academy, and a global network of sister clubs under the City Football Group. These moves were aimed at not just immediate success, but at building a sustainable model for long-term dominance in football. The recruitment strategy was meticulous, focusing on players who fit the City ethos and style of play, complemented by a management team that was forward-thinking and adaptive.

The arrival of Pep Guardiola in 2016 was a pivotal moment in Manchester City's tactical evolution. Guardiola, known for his innovative approach and emphasis on possession-based football, took City's play to new heights. Under his guidance, City adopted a fluid, attacking style that was both mesmerizing to watch and devastatingly effective. The team's tactical flexibility allowed them to dominate possession, control games, and dismantle opponents with precision. Guardiola's influence extended beyond tactics; he instilled a winning mentality and a culture of excellence that permeated every level of the club. The result was a team that played with creativity, cohesion, and an unrelenting desire to win.

As Manchester City's fortunes rose, the dynamics of the Manchester Derby underwent a significant shift. Gone were the days when City was viewed as the underdog; the derby became a clash of titans, with both teams vying not just for local bragging rights, but for supremacy on a global stage. The rivalry intensified, with each encounter marked by high stakes and the world's attention. The derbies became more than just football matches; they were showcases of the city's footballing identity, split between the red of United and the sky blue of City. The rise of Manchester City added a new chapter to the derby's history, transforming it into one of the most anticipated fixtures in the football calendar.

Manchester City's rise is a compelling chapter in modern football. It's a story of ambition realized, where strategic investments, innovative tactics, and a culture of excellence propelled a club from the shadows into the spotlight. As City continues to build on their success, their journey serves as a blueprint for transformation, illustrating that with the right vision, investment, and leadership, even the loftiest dreams can be achieved.

4

THE MIRACLE OF ISTANBUL: LIVERPOOL'S 2005 CHAMPIONS LEAGUE VICTORY

The 2005 Champions League final in Istanbul stands as one of football's most unforgettable nights, a testament to the unpredictability and sheer drama the sport offers. Liverpool, facing AC Milan, found themselves in a seemingly insurmountable position at halftime, trailing by three goals. Yet, what unfolded in the second half and beyond threw this match into the record books of football history.

On that fateful night in Istanbul, as AC Milan's players walked off the pitch at halftime, the scoreline read a comfortable 3-0 in their favor. Liverpool, on the other hand, were staring down the barrel of a humiliating defeat. Fans and pundits had already begun to write them off. However, the second half showcased why football is often dubbed a game of two halves. In a span of six magical minutes, Liverpool turned the tide, drawing level through goals from Steven Gerrard, Vladimir Smicer, and Xabi Alonso. This remarkable comeback under the floodlights of the Atatürk Olympic Stadium is now a cornerstone of football folklore, symbolizing hope and the never-say-die spirit.

Rafael Benitez, Liverpool's tactician, was instrumental in orchestrating what appeared to many as the impossible. Recognizing the need for change, Benitez adjusted his formation and made key substitutions that altered the game's dynamics. By introducing Dietmar Hamann, Benitez fortified his midfield, allowing Gerrard to push forward. This tactical shift disrupted Milan's rhythm and provided Liverpool with the platform they needed to launch their comeback. Benitez's decisions showcased his adeptness at reading the game and his ability to inspire his team to exploit their opponent's vulnerabilities.

The mental fortitude displayed by Liverpool's squad to overcome a three-goal deficit against one of Europe's elite teams cannot go unnoticed. This resilience was not born in the spur of the moment but was cultivated throughout their Champions League campaign. Faced with the daunting task of overturning the deficit, Liverpool's players rallied, driven by a belief in their abilities and trust in one another. This psychological toughness was epitomized by Gerrard's leadership on the pitch, inspiring his teammates to believe that the night was far from over.

The victory in Istanbul transcended the confines of a typical football match, embedding itself in Liverpool's rich history. For fans around the globe, "Istanbul" became synonymous with hope, belief, and the power of collective will. It served as a reminder that in football, as in life, no obstacle is too great when hearts and minds are aligned. The Miracle of Istanbul has since inspired countless players and fans, reinforcing the idea that with grit and determination, the improbable can become possible.

In writing about the Miracle of Istanbul, it's crucial to

capture not just the events as they unfolded but the emotional journey experienced by players and fans alike. This story is a vivid illustration of football's ability to inspire, unite, and provide moments of sheer joy and disbelief. As you recount this chapter in Liverpool's history, consider the broader themes of resilience, tactical ingenuity, and the transformative power of belief. These elements contribute to the enduring legacy of that night in Istanbul, a legacy that continues to resonate with football enthusiasts around the world.

5

SOCCEROOS' LEAP OF FAITH: AUSTRALIA'S 2006 WORLD CUP JOURNEY

In 2006, the Socceroos, as the Australian national football team is affectionately known, ended a drought that had lasted for 32 years, marking their return to the FIFA World Cup stage. This wasn't just a sporting achievement; it was a moment tattooed in the collective memory of a nation, signaling a new dawn for football in Australia. The path to Germany was fraught with challenges, but through sheer determination and a collective leap of faith, the Socceroos not only made it to the tournament but also left an indelible mark with their spirited performances.

The road to Germany for the Socceroos was anything but straightforward. The qualifying rounds were a rollercoaster of emotions, culminating in a nail-biting playoff against Uruguay. The tension in the air during the penalty shootout was palpable, with every Australian holding their breath. When John Aloisi scored the decisive penalty, a nation erupted in joy, and a weight lifted off the shoulders of Australian football. This victory was more than just a ticket to the World Cup; it was redemption, a testament to the resilience and tenacity of the players and the unwavering support of their fans.

Arriving in Germany, the Socceroos were not expected to make waves. Drawn into a group with football powerhouses, they were the quintessential underdogs. Yet, what transpired on the field was a display of courage, skill, and an indomitable spirit that took many by surprise. Their opening match victory against Japan, achieved with a stunning comeback, was a statement of intent. Against Brazil, despite a defeat, the Socceroos played with a level of grit and determination that earned them respect on the world stage. It was in their match against Croatia, however, that the true Aussie spirit shone brightest, securing a draw that propelled them into the knockout stages for the first time in their history.

The Socceroos' campaign in the 2006 World Cup did more than just advance Australia's standing in international football; it ignited a sense of national pride. Across cities and towns, Australians rallied behind their team, waking up at odd hours to catch the live broadcasts. The sight of the green and gold, whether on flags, jerseys, or painted faces, became ubiquitous, symbolizing a collective embrace of the game. This period marked a shift in the national sports psyche, with football claiming its place in the heart of Australian sports culture.

The legacy of the Socceroos' 2006 World Cup journey is multifaceted, impacting not just the players and fans but the broader landscape of football in Australia. In the years that followed, there was a noticeable increase in the popularity of the sport at grassroots levels. Children inspired by the heroics of Tim Cahill, Harry Kewell, and Mark Viduka flocked to local clubs, eager to emulate their idols. The A-League, Australia's premier football competition, saw a surge in interest, with higher attendances and a growing fan base.

Moreover, the success of the national team on the world stage helped to elevate the profile of Australian football internationally. It opened doors for Australian players in leagues around the globe, enhancing the country's reputation as a breeding ground for talented footballers. The investments in youth development, coaching, and infrastructure intensified, driven by a collective ambition to build on the foundations laid by the 2006 World Cup team.

This chapter in Australian football history is a poignant reminder of the transformative power of sport. The Socceroos' leap of faith in 2006 not only brought them to the world's biggest football stage but also brought the game into the hearts and homes of millions of Australians. It was a journey that went beyond the white lines of the pitch. It inspired a nation to dream big and believe in the impossible.

6

ZIDANE'S HEADBUTT: A MOMENT OF MADNESS

Zinedine Zidane's career is filled with moments of brilliance that have cemented his status as one of the game's all-time greats. His vision on the field, his unmatched skill in controlling the ball, and his ability to perform under pressure made him a hero to millions. Yet, even the brightest stars have moments they wish they could erase, instances that remind us of their humanity.

The 2006 World Cup final in Berlin was supposed to be Zidane's swansong, the final act of a glittering career. France faced Italy in a match that had fans around the world on the edge of their seats. As the game progressed, tension mounted, and in a moment that shocked viewers worldwide, Zidane headbutted Italian defender Marco Materazzi in the chest, leading to a red card and expulsion from the game. This act, born out of a verbal provocation, became one of the most talked-about moments in World Cup history, overshadowing the match itself, which Italy went on to win in a penalty shootout.

Before this incident, Zidane had achieved almost everything a footballer could dream of. His career highlights include winning the FIFA World Cup in 1998, where he scored twice in the final against Brazil, leading France to their first-ever World Cup victory. He also won the UEFA Champions League with Real Madrid, a feat punctuated by his stunning volley in the 2002 final against Bayer Leverkusen, considered one of the greatest goals in the competition's history. Zidane's ability to perform in crucial moments, coupled with his elegant style of play, earned him numerous accolades, including the FIFA World Player of the Year award three times.

The headbutt incident, while shocking, adds a layer of complexity to Zidane's legacy rather than tarnishing it outright. It highlights the intense pressure athletes face and the split-second decisions that can define careers. For many fans, Zidane's actions that day did little to diminish their admiration for his contributions to the sport. Instead, it humanized him, adding a chapter of vulnerability to the story of a man who had otherwise seemed invincible on the pitch. Discussions about Zidane's career often include this moment, not as a focal point but as a footnote, a reminder that even legends have flaws.

Footballers, especially those playing at the highest level, are under constant scrutiny, with their every move analyzed and critiqued. The expectation to perform consistently at peak levels, to be role models, and to handle provocations with grace is immense. Zidane's headbutt serves as a case study in the psychological demands of professional football, where the mental resilience required is as crucial as physical fitness and technical skill.

This pressure cooker environment, where emotions run high, and the stakes are even higher, is a breeding ground for moments of intense drama. It underscores the need for mental health support and coping mechanisms for athletes, who must navigate not only the physical demands of their sport but also the psychological and emotional challenges that come with it.

Zidane's moment of madness in the 2006 World Cup final adds to the incredible stories that soccer creates. It shows us that football, for all its glory and spectacle, is a game played by humans, each with their own strengths, weaknesses, and breaking points.

7

THE FALL AND RISE OF AC MILAN

AC Milan, with its long history of victories in iconic red and black jerseys, has long been synonymous with footballing excellence. The club's illustrious past is dotted with periods of unparalleled success, both in Italy and on the European stage. Their trophy cabinet, brimming with domestic league titles, Coppa Italia trophies, and numerous European Cups, stands as a testament to their historical dominance. Milan's legacy is not just built on victories but on the way they achieved them - with style, grace, and a commitment to the beautiful game.

However, even the mightiest of giants can stumble, and AC Milan's story took a turn as the club faced challenges that saw them drift from the pinnacle of European football. The decline was gradual, a confluence of aging stars, managerial changes, and financial constraints that saw the Rossoneri's grip on Italian and European football loosen. The once intimidating force at the San Siro found it increasingly difficult to compete at the highest level, with their absence from the UEFA Champions League becoming a glaring indicator of their fall from grace.

The path to redemption for AC Milan involved a comprehensive reassessment of their strategy, both on and off the pitch. The club's leadership recognized the need for a structured rebuilding effort, focusing on financial stability, youth development, and a clear footballing philosophy. This involved making tough decisions, including parting ways with high-wage veterans to make room for budding talent and a more sustainable wage structure. Milan also invested in their scouting network, aiming to uncover and nurture young talents who could carry the club's legacy into the future.

The cornerstone of Milan's revival has been a renewed focus on youth and resilience. The club's academy, long a source of pride, began to take center stage as Milan looked to its own ranks to provide the energy and passion needed to drive the first team forward. Players like Gianluigi Donnarumma and Davide Calabria, both academy graduates, became symbols of this new era, embodying the blend of talent and determination that Milan's strategy aimed to foster.

In parallel, the club's management made strategic signings that complemented their youth-centric approach. The acquisition of players not necessarily at the zenith of their careers but with potential and room to grow became a hallmark of Milan's transfer strategy. This approach required patience from the fans and trust in the club's vision, elements that were gradually rewarded as the team's performances began to improve.

The coaching carousel that had plagued Milan in their years of decline began to slow, with the club offering a more stable environment for managerial talent to thrive and implement long-term visions. The appointment of Stefano Pioli, initially seen as a stop-gap measure, turned into a catalyst for change as he fostered a spirit of unity and a clear tactical identity within the squad.

As Milan continues to rebuild, the landscape of modern football presents both challenges and opportunities for the storied club. The financial might of clubs across Europe, fueled by wealthy owners and lucrative broadcasting deals, means Milan faces stiff competition in the transfer market and in holding onto their brightest talents. However, Milan's rich history and the allure of playing for such a prestigious club remain powerful tools in attracting talent.

The Rossoneri's resurgence is also timed with the evolution of football into a more global sport. Milan's brand, recognized worldwide, positions them well to capitalize on emerging markets and fanbases, broadening their commercial appeal and opening new revenue streams to compete financially at the highest level.

The integration of technology in football, from data analytics in scouting and performance analysis to fan engagement through digital platforms, offers Milan avenues to regain their edge. By embracing innovation in sports science, tactical analysis, and global branding, Milan can once again assert themselves as leaders in the football world.

Moreover, the passionate Milanese fans, who have stood by the club through thick and thin, remain the heartbeat of AC Milan. Their support, unwavering even in the darkest times, will be crucial as the club seeks to reclaim its place among football's elite. The shared dream of seeing Milan return to the pinnacle of European nights, competing for the highest honors, is a powerful motivator for all associated with the club.

As AC Milan navigates the complexities of modern football, their journey from decline to resurgence serves as a compelling story of resilience, strategic foresight, and the enduring power of community. The path ahead is lined with challenges, but for a club with Milan's history and spirit, the pursuit of greatness is an ever-present goal, driving them forward in the ever-evolving landscape of the beautiful game.

8

AJAX'S YOUTH REVOLUTION: BREEDING GROUND OF LEGENDS

At the heart of Amsterdam, where the canals intersect with the dreams of aspiring footballers, stands a club whose name resonates far beyond its geographic confines. Ajax Amsterdam, with its storied history and iconic red and white jerseys, is not just a football club; it's an institution that has consistently been at the forefront of nurturing world-class talent. The philosophy here is simple yet profoundly impactful: invest in youth, and the youth will invest in your future success.

Ajax operates on a belief system that champions the growth and development of young players, instilling in them not only the skills required to excel on the pitch but also the values necessary to thrive off it. This philosophy is deeply embedded in the club's DNA, tracing back to the visionary Johan Cruyff, whose ideas about football and player development reshaped Ajax's approach to the game. At the core of this philosophy lies the renowned Ajax Youth Academy, De Toekomst, or 'The Future', a fitting name for a facility that symbolizes hope and the promise of tomorrow.

The academy's approach is holistic, focusing on technical skills, tactical understanding, physical fitness, and psychological resilience. Young talents are taught the importance of playing an attractive, attacking brand of football, reminiscent of the Total Football that Ajax is famous for. This emphasis on all-round development ensures that graduates from the academy are not just footballers but ambassadors of the Ajax way, ready to face the challenges of professional football.

The fruits of Ajax's youth development system are evident in the constellation of stars that have graced the world stage. Players like Johan Cruyff, Dennis Bergkamp, and more recently, Matthijs de Ligt and Frenkie de Jong, are testaments to the academy's success. These players, who went on to achieve greatness both domestically and internationally, share a common origin: the training fields of De Toekomst. Their careers serve as inspiration for every new generation that walks through the academy's gates, dreaming of following in their footsteps.

The influence of Ajax's youth development philosophy extends far beyond the confines of Amsterdam or even the Netherlands. Football clubs around the world look to Ajax as a model for building and sustaining a successful youth academy. The club's approach to nurturing talent, emphasizing technical skill, and playing a proactive style of football has inspired many clubs to invest more significantly in their youth systems. This ripple effect has led to a broader appreciation for the long-term benefits of developing players internally, rather than relying solely on the transfer market for team building.

Moreover, Ajax's success on the European stage, notably their runs in the UEFA Champions League, has showcased the potential of teams built around homegrown talent. Their philosophy challenges the prevailing trend of heavy spending in football, offering an alternative path to success that is both sustainable and deeply rewarding.

Despite its successes, Ajax faces numerous challenges in the modern football landscape, dominated by financial powerhouses. The club operates in a market where retaining top talent becomes increasingly difficult, as richer clubs often lure away young stars with the promise of higher wages and greater exposure. This reality necessitates a constant cycle of development, where the departure of one generation paves the way for the next.

To stay competitive, Ajax has adapted its strategy, focusing on international scouting to supplement its academy intake and investing in state-of-the-art facilities to enhance player development. The club has also become adept at navigating the transfer market, reinvesting proceeds from player sales into both the academy and strategic acquisitions to maintain competitiveness.

In facing these challenges, Ajax remains committed to its core philosophy, viewing each obstacle as an opportunity to innovate and evolve. The club's resilience in the face of change, coupled with its dedication to youth development, ensures that Ajax Amsterdam will continue to be a producer of talent for many years to come.

In this era where the business of football often overshadows the game itself, Ajax's youth revolution stands as a reminder of the sport's true essence: the joy of playing, the purity of growth, and the dreams of those who dare to imagine a future draped in the colors of their beloved club. It's a testament to the belief that with the right foundations, nurturing environments, and a commitment to principles, success is not just attainable but sustainable. As the world of football continues to evolve, the story of Ajax and its youth development system will undoubtedly serve as an enduring story of inspiration, challenging clubs worldwide to rethink the way they approach the beautiful game.

9

THE SENEGAL LIONS' ROAR: 2002 WORLD CUP ODYSSEY

In the football history books, the 2002 World Cup stands out not just for the unexpected results and the drama on the pitch but for the emergence of heroes from corners of the world football had yet to shine its brightest lights on. Among these, the tale of Senegal's Lions stands tall and proud, a story that resonates deep in the heart of Africa and beyond, proving that in football, giants can be both born and toppled in the span of 90 minutes.

The stage was the world's most prestigious tournament, and the actors, a Senegalese team making their debut on this grand platform. Few outside their homeland gave them a chance; they were, after all, pitted against some of the most illustrious national teams in the world. Yet, as the tournament unfolded, it became clear that the Lions of Teranga, as they are affectionately known, were not there to make up the numbers. Each match was a display of their tenacity, skill, and an indomitable will to succeed against the odds. Their journey to the quarter-finals was not just a series of football matches; it was a tale of underdogs rising to the occasion, challenging norms, and rewriting their destiny on the global stage.

The highlight of Senegal's remarkable run was undoubtedly their opening match against France, the then-defending champions and one of the favorites to win the tournament. The encounter was more than a game; it was a David versus Goliath battle, a test of spirit, and a clash of histories. When Papa Bouba Diop scored the only goal of the match, it was not just Senegal celebrating; it was a moment of triumph for underdogs everywhere. This victory was more than an upset; it set the tone for Senegal's campaign, instilling a belief in the team and its supporters that this World Cup could be a stage for their dreams to unfold.

Senegal's performance in the tournament captured the imagination of fans around the world and became a symbol of African football's potential and promise. In a sport where European and South American teams have historically dominated, the Lions' roar was a reminder of the talent, passion, and spirit that thrived in Africa. Their run to the quarter-finals was not just a victory for Senegal but a victory for African football, showcasing the continent's ability to compete at the highest level. This achievement was a beacon of hope and pride for millions, highlighting the rich footballing talent in Africa waiting for its moment in the sun.

The impact of the 2002 World Cup on Senegal and its players was profound and lasting. On the streets of Dakar and beyond, children donned the national team's jersey, playing football with dreams of emulating their heroes. The success of the team was a catalyst for the development of the sport in the country, leading to increased investment in football infrastructure, youth development, and the domestic league. The players who starred in the tournament became legends, their careers a source of inspiration for future generations.

For the likes of El Hadji Diouf, Papa Bouba Diop, and Khalilou Fadiga, the tournament was a launching pad to greater heights in their professional careers. Their performances on the world stage opened doors to opportunities in Europe's top leagues, where they continued to excel and pave the way for fellow Senegalese players. The legacy of this team, however, transcends individual achievements. It's etched in the collective memory of a nation and a continent, serving as a poignant reminder of what can be accomplished with belief, unity, and the courage to dream.

The 2002 World Cup odyssey of the Senegal Lions is more than a chapter in football history; it's a story of breaking barriers, challenging preconceptions, and the pure, unadulterated joy of competing on the world's biggest stage. It's a story that continues to inspire, reminding us of the power of sport to unite, to excite, and to create heroes out of the unlikely.

10

MOHAMED SALAH: EGYPTIAN KING

This is the tale of Mohamed Salah, known affectionately as the Egyptian King. Salah's story isn't just about football; it's a spark that lights up dreams, challenges stereotypes, and gives back generously, inspiring a whole continent along the way.

Imagine a young boy from Nagrig, a small village in Egypt, with a football at his feet and a dream in his heart. His name is Mohamed Salah. Every day, he faced a grueling five-hour round trip to train with El Mokawloon, a Cairo club. This wasn't just a journey across miles; it was a relentless pursuit of a dream amidst countless challenges. Salah's path wasn't paved with gold but with determination and sacrifice. His early career took him from the Swiss club Basel to Chelsea, then on loan to Fiorentina and Roma, before finally joining Liverpool. At each step, he honed his skills, his resolve solid as the pyramids back home. Today, Salah stands among the premier footballers of the world, a testament to the fact that where you come from does not dictate where you can go.

Salah's impact goes beyond the white lines of the

pitch. In a world quick to form stereotypes, he emerges as a figure challenging preconceived notions about Muslims. His celebrations - often a sujood, a Muslim act of prostration - speak of his faith proudly in the global spotlight of the Premier League. This subtle act of faith, combined with his demeanor on and off the pitch, has endeared him to fans worldwide, fostering a dialogue about inclusivity and understanding. Salah's story is a reminder that heroes come in all forms, smashing barriers and building bridges in communities.

"He who sleeps with a full stomach whilst his neighbor goes hungry is not one of us." This saying resonates deeply with Salah, who has never forgotten his roots amidst his success. His contributions to Nagrig and Egypt are legendary - from funding medical facilities and schools to regular donations that support families in his hometown. Salah's philanthropy extends beyond financial aid; it's a lifeline that uplifts communities, providing hope and opportunities where they are needed most. His commitment to giving back is a beacon of how success is not just about lifting oneself but lifting those around you.

Salah's legacy is a beacon for aspiring footballers in Egypt and across Africa. He's shattered the glass ceiling, showing that talent, hard work, and perseverance can lead to global acclaim. Young athletes in dusty fields across the continent now have a living example that their dreams are valid, that they too can grace the world's biggest stages. Salah has inspired a new generation to pursue their passion for football, proving that heroes don't just exist in stories; they emerge from the very fields they once played on as children.

11

THE ITALIAN STALLION: FRANCESCO TOTTI'S ROMA LOVE AFFAIR

In the heart of Rome, amidst the echoes of its ancient glory, emerged a footballer whose tale is not just synonymous with AS Roma but it's ingrained in the very soul of the city.

Francesco Totti, the Italian Stallion, is more than a football legend; he is the embodiment of loyalty, a rarity in the modern game's transitory nature.

Totti's bond with Roma is a story of devotion. In an age where the allure of wealth and trophies often tempts players away, Totti's career stands as a monument to fidelity. His journey with Roma began at the tender age of 13. Over the years, the whispers of interest from football's giants were constant. Yet, Totti, with the Colosseum's steadfastness, remained loyal to his city, his club, and his people. This unwavering allegiance elevated him from a mere player to the eternal captain in the hearts of the Giallorossi faithful.

Totti's career is a mosaic of unforgettable moments, each a brushstroke in his masterpiece with Roma. One cannot forget the audacity of his cucchiaio, a delicate chip, against Inter Milan, a moment of pure inventiveness that sent the Stadio Olimpico into raptures. Then there's the record-breaking penalty against Torino, making him Serie A's second-highest scorer of all time. Each goal, each celebration, was a testament to his genius, a player whose creativity knew no bounds and whose leadership lifted those around him.

Totti transcends the realm of football, becoming a symbol of Rome itself. His image adorns murals in the city's labyrinthine alleys, a testament to his impact beyond the pitch. Totti represents the spirit of Rome, its resilience, and its heart. His commitment to the city's club in the face of tempting offers from abroad speaks volumes of his character, embodying the Roman virtue of loyalty. His presence at charity events, his engagement with the city's youth, and his outspoken love for Rome have intertwined his legacy with the city's cultural fabric.

The legacy of Francesco Totti is a beacon for aspiring athletes and a reminder of the profound impact a player can have on a club and its supporters. His career serves as a story of passion, illustrating that the essence of football lies not in the trophies or the accolades but in the love for the game and one's club. Future generations of players look to Totti not just for his skill on the ball but for his embodiment of loyalty, a rare virtue that endears him to fans worldwide. His tale encourages players to forge connections with their clubs that resonate on a deeper level, transcending the boundaries of the sport.

Totti's journey with Roma is a poignant chapter in football's vast saga, highlighting the beauty of loyalty in an ever-changing sport. His character reflects the values that endear football to millions, reminding us that at its core, the game is about passion, commitment, and an unbreakable bond with one's roots.

12

DIDIER DROGBA: UNITING A NATION THROUGH FOOTBALL

In the sprawling world of football, few stories resonate as powerfully or poignantly as that of Didier Drogba. His story weaves through the heart of conflict, dances on the grand stages of club success, and writes chapters of generosity that transform communities. But perhaps most significantly, Drogba's legacy is one of leadership—a beacon guiding others through storms, both on the field and off.

In a moment that transcends the sport itself, Drogba's voice became the rallying cry for peace in his home country, Ivory Coast. Amidst a backdrop of civil war tearing the nation apart, Drogba's plea for unity did not just echo; it penetrated the hearts of millions. Following a match-winning performance that secured Ivory Coast's place in the 2006 World Cup, Drogba knelt with his teammates, making a heartfelt appeal to combatants on live television. His courage to use his platform for peace sparked a cease-fire, proving the remarkable power of sports as a unifying force. Drogba's actions remind us that athletes hold in their grasp not just the power to entertain but to heal and unite.

Drogba's legacy at Chelsea FC is the stuff of legends, woven into the fabric of the club's history. His tenure in London was marked by relentless pursuit of victory, epitomized by his critical role in Chelsea's 2012 Champions League triumph. Drogba was not merely a player; he was a warrior, embodying the spirit and determination that propelled Chelsea to its greatest heights. His equalizing header in the final against Bayern Munich, followed by the decisive penalty in the shoot-out, secured Chelsea's first Champions League title. These moments are immortalized in the memories of fans, a testament to Drogba's indomitable spirit.

Drogba's influence stretches far beyond the football pitch, into realms where hope is a scarce commodity. Through the Didier Drogba Foundation, he has spearheaded efforts to improve healthcare and education across Africa, focusing on building hospitals, clinics, and schools. His commitment to philanthropy is driven by a belief in empowerment through education and health, laying the groundwork for a brighter future for countless individuals. Drogba's endeavors reflect a profound understanding that true success is measured not in trophies or accolades but in lives touched and communities uplifted.

Drogba's journey is a story rich with tales of victory, resilience, and generosity, but its core is leadership. His ability to inspire those around him, to stand as a beacon of hope in times of turmoil, and to wield his influence for the greater good marks him as a true leader. This legacy is not confined to the realms of football; it transcends into the broader sphere of global influence, where Drogba continues to advocate for peace, unity, and development.

His leadership extends a challenge to others, inviting athletes and individuals alike to leverage their platforms for positive change, echoing the idea that every action, every word, can ripple through society, altering the course of history.

Drogba's story teaches us that heroes are made not just by their feats on the battlefield of sport but by their capacity to lead, to give, and to unite. In a world often divided, his legacy serves as a reminder of the profound impact one individual can have, inspiring generations to come not only to dream but to act with courage, compassion, and conviction.

13

SUNIL CHHETRI: THE INDIAN FOOTBALL DREAM

In a nation where cricket is often considered the only sport worth following, Sunil Chhetri stands as a towering figure, challenging this notion with every goal, every match, and every victory. His story is not just about personal glory but about placing Indian football on the world's map, making the beautiful game impossible to ignore in a cricket-crazed country.

Chhetri's rise is a story of resilience and passion. From the dusty fields of Delhi to the green pitches of international stadiums, his journey has been an uphill battle, fighting not just opponents but the very culture of sports fandom in India. Yet, with each goal, Chhetri has carved a niche for football in the hearts of millions, introducing the thrill of the game to a new audience. His achievements with the national team and clubs abroad have brought attention to Indian football, showcasing the talent and potential that lies within the country.

Leadership is innate to Chhetri. On and off the pitch, his presence uplifts the team, fans, and even the sport itself within India. His call to fans, urging them to support the national team in stadiums, wasn't just a plea; it was a rallying cry that filled seats and hearts. Chhetri leads by example, demonstrating that dedication and hard work can elevate not just an individual but an entire team, inspiring both his teammates and young athletes across the nation.

Chhetri's name is etched in the record books, not just in India but internationally. Just behind Lionel Messi as one of the highest active international goal scorers is a feat that speaks volumes of his skill, perseverance, and knack for finding the back of the net. This achievement has not only brought pride to India but has also placed Indian football in a new light on the global stage, challenging stereotypes and showcasing the quality of footballers the country can produce.

Chhetri's vision extends beyond his personal achievements; he is deeply invested in the future of Indian football. His involvement in youth development is a testament to his commitment to nurturing the next generation of footballers. Chhetri understands that for Indian football to flourish, it must build from the ground up, providing children with the facilities, coaching, and opportunities to pursue their dreams. His advocacy for better infrastructure and support systems is driven by a belief in the untapped potential of Indian youth, waiting for a chance to shine on the football field.

Sunil Chhetri's story is more than just about his accomplishments as a footballer; it's a beacon for the aspirations of a nation discovering its love for football. Through his journey, leadership, records, and advocacy, Chhetri is not just scoring goals; he's scoring points for the future of Indian football, ensuring that the beautiful game finds its rightful place in the hearts of a billion.

14

THE RESILIENCE OF CHAPECOENSE

In the realm of football, stories of triumph and heartache paint the vast canvas with emotions that resonate universally. Amidst this rich history, the tale of Chapecoense emerges, not merely as a story of a football club but as a poignant reminder of the human spirit's resilience. This story unfolds in the tragic shadow of a catastrophic event, yet it's illuminated by the enduring light of hope, solidarity, and rebirth.

The serene night of November 28, 2016, was pierced by the news that shook the football world to its core. Chapecoense, a Brazilian football club that had captured the hearts of many with its Cinderella story, faced an unimaginable tragedy. A plane carrying the team to the Copa Sudamericana final in Colombia crashed, claiming the lives of 71 people, including players, staff, and journalists. The world stood still as the news unfolded, a stark reminder of how fleeting life can be. But from this abyss of despair, Chapecoense found a way to forge a path towards healing and rebuilding. The club's decision to continue, to honor those lost by pressing forward, became a testament to the indomitable spirit that defines football and humanity alike.

In the wake of the crash, a wave of solidarity swept across the football community. Clubs, players, and fans worldwide extended their support to Chapecoense, embodying the unspoken bond that unites the football family in times of sorrow. Offers of assistance poured in, from loaning players without fees to financial support, each gesture reinforcing the notion that some things transcend rivalry and competition. This global outpouring of empathy and solidarity was a silver lining, highlighting the compassion and unity that football can inspire.

Chapecoense's return to competitive football was a journey marked by tears, triumphs, and, above all, resilience. Their first match after the tragedy was charged with emotions. Each game played was a step towards healing, a tribute to those who had dreamt of lifting the Copa Sudamericana trophy. The club's performance in the subsequent seasons, against the backdrop of their profound loss, was nothing short of heroic. Qualifying for international competitions and securing vital wins in the league, Chapecoense demonstrated that their spirit remained unbroken, a show of hope and determination against the odds.

The club has become a symbol of hope, not just for the city of Chapecó but for the world. The legacy of those lost in the tragedy continues to inspire, a reminder of the preciousness of life and the power of community in the face of unimaginable loss. Chapecoense's journey from tragedy to triumph is a testament to the fact that even in the darkest moments, light can be found, and from despair, strength can emerge.

The story of Chapecoense is woven into the fabric of

football folklore. The club's saga, marked by heartache and triumph, continues to inspire, a poignant reminder that even in the darkest times, hope endures, and from the ashes of despair, new beginnings can arise.

15

THE GOLDEN GENERATION: BELGIUM'S RISE

The emergence of a "Golden Generation" in any country is a rare phenomenon. A confluence of talent, timing, and vision that transforms a nation's footballing destiny. Belgium's ascension to the zenith of world football is a story that captures this rare alignment, marked by the rise of players who would redefine the Red Devils' place in the global game.

The unveiling of Belgium's "Golden Generation" was not an overnight sensation but a gradual revelation, as stars like Eden Hazard and Kevin De Bruyne stepped onto the world stage. These players, along with others such as Romelu Lukaku and Thibaut Courtois, emerged from Belgium's youth systems and clubs abroad, showcasing a blend of skill, creativity, and tactical intelligence that was both refreshing and formidable. Hazard's dribbling wizardry and De Bruyne's pinpoint passing became the hallmark of a team brimming with potential, setting the stage for Belgium's assault on football's highest bastions.

The 2018 World Cup in Russia was the crucible where Belgium's golden cohort was tested, a tournament that saw them reaching the semi-finals, their finest achievement on this stage to date. The journey was punctuated by moments of brilliance, tactical nous, and resilience. A memorable victory against Brazil in the quarter-finals showcased Belgium's tactical flexibility and mental fortitude, attributes that underscored their campaign. However, it was the semi-final against France that offered the sternest test, a match that, despite ending in defeat, solidified Belgium's status as a footballing powerhouse and a team of undeniable talent and heart.

The roots of Belgium's golden era can be traced back to a comprehensive overhaul of their youth development programs in the late 1990s and early 2000s. Recognizing the need for systemic change, the Belgian Football Association, along with clubs across the country, implemented reforms aimed at improving coaching standards, facilities, and the overall approach to youth football. A focus on technical skills, cognitive development, and a holistic view of the player's growth became the cornerstone of these reforms. This long-term vision for nurturing talent was instrumental in producing the players who would go on to dazzle the world.

The legacy of Belgium's golden generation extends beyond their achievements on the pitch; it sets a precedent and a blueprint for the future. The challenge now is to sustain this level of excellence, ensuring that the pipeline of talent remains robust and that the national team continues to compete at the highest levels. The pressure to live up to the golden generation's legacy is immense, yet it is also a motivating force, driving young players, coaches, and the footballing infrastructure to strive for continued success. The impact of this generation on

Belgium's footballing culture is indelible, inspiring future stars to dream big and aim high.

The story of Belgium's rise is a testament to the power of vision, investment in youth, and the emergence of a generation of players who have redefined what is possible for a small nation on football's global stage. Their legacy is not just in the matches won or the accolades earned but in the inspiration they provide to the next generation, ensuring that the flame of Belgian football burns bright long into the future.

16

THE DANISH DYNAMITE: DENMARK'S 1992 EUROPEAN TRIUMPH

In international football history, some stories stand out not for the expected victories by powerhouse nations but for the tales of unexpected glory that captivate the hearts of fans worldwide. Among these, the story of Denmark's victory at the 1992 European Championship stands out and shows the unpredictable nature of football. This victory wasn't scripted in the stars nor predicted by pundits; it was a tale of serendipity, unity, and strategic brilliance that propelled Denmark from a last-minute entrant to European champions.

Denmark's journey to the 1992 European Championship was nothing short of a fairy tale. Not initially qualified for the tournament, the Danish Dynamites found themselves packing for Sweden only after Yugoslavia's unfortunate disqualification. With scant preparation and modest expectations from the footballing world, Denmark was thrust into a group with France, England, and Sweden - teams with far greater expectations and preparations under their belts. This twist of fate set the stage for what was to become one of the most remarkable underdog stories in football history.

What Denmark lacked in preparation time, they more than made up for with an unbreakable bond and team spirit. This unity was the squad's backbone, turning a group of talented individuals into a formidable collective force. The Danish team, led by the inspirational Lars Olsen and buoyed by the brilliance of the Laudrup brothers, showcased a camaraderie that seemed to grow stronger with each game. Each player knew their role, each man fought for his brother on the pitch, and it was this bond that saw them through matches that many had expected would be their downfall. In the semi-finals against the Netherlands and the finals against Germany, Denmark's unity was palpable, a visible force that drove them to outperform and outlast teams that were, on paper, far superior.

The mastermind behind Denmark's tactical approach was coach Richard Møller Nielsen, a figure who, until then, had been relatively unknown on the international stage. Møller Nielsen's tactical ingenuity lay in his ability to adapt his strategies to the strengths and weaknesses of his opponents, making astute observations and adjustments that often caught the opposition off guard. His defensive tactics, reliance on swift counter-attacks, and the freedom he gave his players to express themselves on the pitch were pivotal in Denmark's success. The coach's pragmatic approach to each game, coupled with his trust in his players' abilities and the team's unity, created a tactical balance that proved unbeatable during the tournament.

The long-lasting impact of Denmark's 1992 triumph on the nation and European football cannot be overstated. For Denmark, this victory was more than just a sporting achievement; it was a moment of national pride that united the country and showcased the potential of Danish football on the world stage. The Danish Dynamites became household names, heroes who had defied the odds to bring glory to their homeland.

For European football, Denmark's win was a reminder of the sport's unpredictable nature and the fact that underdogs, with the right mix of talent, unity, and tactical awareness, could triumph against the odds. The legacy of this victory continues to inspire smaller footballing nations with the belief that, on their day, they can compete with and beat the best in the world. Denmark's 1992 European Championship win remains one of the most inspirational stories in football, a testament to the fact that in football, as in life, anything is possible.

17

JAPAN'S WOMEN WARRIORS: 2011 WORLD CUP VICTORY

In the heart of every football fan lies a deep-seated belief in miracles — moments that defy expectations and bring about joy unparalleled. The story of Japan's national women's football team in the 2011 FIFA Women's World Cup is one such tale, marked not by the might of physical strength but by the power of hope, strategy, and indomitable will. Their ascent to glory wasn't scripted in pre-tournament predictions; it was carved out on the pitch, with each match charting a course towards an unprecedented triumph.

The air in Frankfurt on that fateful day of the final carried whispers of anticipation. Up against the United States, a titan in women's football, Japan's Nadeshiko found themselves on the brink of history. The match, a rollercoaster of emotions, saw Japan trailing twice, only to level the scores each time, pushing the contest into penalties. It was here, under the weight of expectation and history, that Japan showcased nerve and precision, clinching the World Cup in a moment that transcended the confines of sport. This victory was not just for the team or the country; it was a moment of inspiration for the entire continent, marking the first time an Asian team had lifted the Women's World Cup.

Months before their World Cup campaign, Japan faced a tragedy of unimaginable proportions. The devastating earthquake and tsunami of March 2011 had left the country in mourning, with the shadow of despair looming large. Amidst this backdrop of sorrow, the Nadeshiko embarked on their World Cup journey, carrying with them the hopes and dreams of a nation yearning for a flicker of joy in trying times. Their triumph, therefore, was more than a sporting victory; it was a testament to resilience, offering a glimmer of happiness and national pride in the face of adversity.

The tactical acumen of coach Norio Sasaki played a pivotal role in Japan's success. Understanding the physical prowess of their opponents, Sasaki devised a strategy that leveraged Japan's strengths — technical skill, quick passing, and tactical discipline. The team's ability to maintain possession, coupled with their adeptness at exploiting spaces with precision and creativity, became their hallmark throughout the tournament. Against teams with a tradition of dominance in women's football, Japan's tactical execution was a masterclass in playing to one's strengths while neutralizing the opposition's.

Japan's victory in the 2011 World Cup did more than write their names in the history books; it served as a catalyst for the growth of women's football globally and in Asia. The triumph shattered ceilings and laid down a marker for the potential of women's football in regions hitherto dominated by their male counterparts. In its wake, the world witnessed a surge in interest and investment in women's football, with leagues around the globe seeing increased visibility and support. Asia, in particular, saw a newfound enthusiasm for the women's game, inspired by the Nadeshiko's journey from underdogs to World Cup champions.

This story of Japan's Women Warriors in the 2011 World Cup is a story that resonates with the soul of football — a saga of triumph against odds, a testament to tactical brilliance, and a beacon of hope in the darkest of times. It's a reminder that in football, miracles don't just happen; they are scripted on the pitch, with determination, strategy, and a heart full of dreams. Unfortunately, I can't fulfill this request.

18

THE HUMBLE KING: KAKA'S JOURNEY OF FAITH

In a world often captivated by the razzmatazz surrounding modern football, Ricardo Izecson dos Santos Leite, widely recognized as Kaka, offers a story that strikes a chord of humility and devotion. His ascent from the bustling streets of Brazil to the iconic San Siro in Milan encapsulates more than just footballing prowess; it embodies a tale of unwavering faith, profound achievements, and altruistic endeavors.

Kaka's path to stardom was set against the vibrant backdrop of Brazilian football, where his extraordinary talent first flickered to life. São Paulo FC, a club with a rich history of nurturing young talents, became the crucible for his early development. Here, Kaka's blend of elegance and explosive power began to draw attention, not just for his ability to glide past defenders with ease but for his knack for decisive playmaking. His meteoric rise caught the eyes of scouts across the globe, setting the stage for a move that would see him don the red and black of AC Milan. At Milan, Kaka transitioned from a promising youngster to a world-class maestro, orchestrating play with an artistry that became the heartbeat of the team. His time in Italy was defined by breathtaking goals, mesmerizing runs, and an innate understanding of the game that endeared him to fans worldwide.

For Kaka, football has always been intertwined with his deep Christian faith, a cornerstone that has guided his life on and off the pitch. He famously displayed a t-shirt that read "I Belong to Jesus" during celebrations, a public declaration of his faith that resonated with many around the world. This spiritual grounding provided Kaka with a sense of purpose and humility, attributes that shone through in his demeanor and interactions. His faith was not just a personal sanctuary but a source of strength that propelled him through the highs and lows of a demanding career.

Kaka's cabinet of accolades is a testament to his impact on the game. His pinnacle at Milan came in 2007 when he lifted the UEFA Champions League trophy, a night that saw him crowned as the competition's top scorer. That same year, Kaka was awarded the Ballon d'Or, cementing his status as the world's best player. These achievements were not merely personal triumphs but milestones that inspired those around him, showcasing the blend of leadership and humility that defines a true champion. Kaka's legacy is punctuated by moments of brilliance that transcended club rivalries, earning him respect and admiration across the football world.

Kaka's journey extends beyond the accolades and the adulation, into realms where football serves as a bridge to change lives. His role as a UN World Food Programme ambassador reflects his commitment to leveraging his platform for a greater good. Through this partnership, Kaka has been at the forefront of initiatives aimed at combating hunger and poverty, echoing his belief in using his influence to make a tangible difference. His philanthropic efforts underscore a legacy that transcends football, embodying the essence of using one's talents and resources to foster hope and create opportunities for those in need.

Kaka's story weaves through the fabric of football, leaving a trail of inspiration, humility, and faith. It's a story that resonates with the purity of the game, reminding us that at its very core, football is about passion, dedication, and the power of dreams fueled by belief. His journey from São Paulo to Milan and beyond serves as a beacon for aspiring athletes, a testament to the notion that while talent can elevate you to the top, it's character that defines your legacy.

19

THE AMERICAN DREAM: CLINT DEMPSEY'S TRAIL FROM TEXAS

In the vast landscape of American sports, where football of a different sort reigns supreme, emerges a tale that captures the essence of the American Dream. This is the story of Clint Dempsey, a boy from Nacogdoches, Texas, who dared to dream beyond the Friday night lights of high school football fame, setting his sights on conquering the global stage of what the rest of the world passionately calls football.

Dempsey's early life was far from the glamorous world of professional sports. Raised in a modest trailer home, the financial challenges his family faced could have easily derailed his aspirations. Yet, it was within these constraints that Dempsey's grit and determination were forged. Sacrifices were made by his family, driving hundreds of miles to ensure he could play in competitive youth leagues, laying the foundation for his unyielding spirit. This part of Dempsey's life is a testament to the power of perseverance, embodying the belief that humble beginnings can indeed lead to illustrious ends.

Dempsey's voyage to the English Premier League

marked a pivotal chapter in his career. Fulham FC, a club with its own tales of defiance, became his home in 2007. In the heart of London, Dempsey blossomed, becoming a fan favorite with his flair, work ethic, and knack for scoring crucial goals. His most memorable moment came in 2010, scoring a jaw-dropping chip against Juventus, a goal that not only sealed a historic comeback but also wrote his name in Fulham folklore. Later, at Tottenham Hotspur, Dempsey continued to showcase his talent, competing at the highest levels and against the best in the game, further solidifying his status as one of the finest American exports to grace the Premier League.

On the international stage, Dempsey donned the stars and stripes with pride, becoming a cornerstone of the United States Men's National Team (USMNT). His contributions were pivotal, from scoring in three FIFA World Cup tournaments to becoming one of the team's all-time leading scorers. Dempsey's leadership and tenacity on the field inspired a generation, playing a crucial role in elevating the profile of soccer in the United States. His legacy with the USMNT is not just measured in goals but in the passion and resilience he brought to every match, setting a standard for future generations to aspire to.

Beyond the accolades and the memorable moments, Dempsey's real impact lies in the inspiration he provides to countless young footballers across the United States and the globe. His journey from a small Texas town to the pinnacle of international soccer breaks down the notion that the American Dream is confined to any one sport or field. Dempsey stands as a symbol of hope, a reminder that with determination, hard work, and a bit of audacity, barriers can be broken, and dreams can be achieved.

Dempsey's story is inspiring for budding athletes, illuminating the path that hard work, sacrifice, and belief in oneself can indeed lead to the realization of one's highest goals. His story resonates not just with those dreaming of a career in soccer but with anyone who faces seemingly insurmountable odds. Clint Dempsey's legacy is a testament to the enduring spirit of the American Dream, a story that continues to inspire and motivate, proving that from modest beginnings can emerge legends that transcend the sport.

20

THE PHOENIX: LANDON DONOVAN'S COMEBACK

Landon Donovan's journey to soccer stardom is a tale of relentless passion and unwavering determination. From the sunlit fields of Southern California to the grand stages of international football, Donovan's rise was fueled by an indomitable spirit. As a young player, his exceptional speed and keen vision set him apart, leading him to the prestigious Bayer Leverkusen at just 16. Though he faced challenges abroad, Donovan's resilience shone brightly upon his return to the U.S., where he became a cornerstone for Major League Soccer.

Donovan's career was marked by moments of pure brilliance—his stunning goals in the World Cup, his crucial role in thrilling MLS Cup victories, and his inspiring leadership both on and off the field. Each chapter of his career added layers to his legacy, not only as a player but as an ambassador of the sport. So it was no surprise that the world was taken aback when he retired.

However, it was Landon Donovan's decision to step back onto the field, after declaring his departure from professional soccer, that marked the biggest chapter of his football career. It was more than a mere return; it was an emblem of his undying love for the game. This act, bold and filled with passion, was not spurred by the desire for accolades or the pursuit of unfinished business on the field. Instead, it was the magnetic pull of soccer, a sport woven into the very fabric of his being, that coaxed Donovan out of retirement. This stage in his life underscores a simple truth: for some, soccer is not just a phase or a career but a lifelong companion.

This return was marked by more than just a physical comeback; it was deeply intertwined with Donovan's journey through mental health struggles. Candid and brave, Donovan shed light on the pressures that athletes often face in silence. His openness about dealing with depression and anxiety peeled back the curtain on the less glamorous side of professional sports, offering solace to many who battle similar demons. It illustrated that even heroes have vulnerabilities and that acknowledging and addressing mental health is a sign of strength, not weakness.

Donovan's impact resonated beyond his prowess on the field; his leadership qualities shone brightly, influencing not just his teammates but the next generation of soccer players. Through coaching roles and involvement in youth soccer initiatives, Donovan committed himself to nurturing emerging talents. His dedication to sharing his knowledge and experiences reflects a legacy that transcends goals and assists. Donovan's journey is a testament to the idea that true leaders continue to inspire and guide, even when they're no longer in the spotlight.

Reflecting on Donovan's return to soccer, it becomes clear that his story is a show of resilience. It serves as a reminder that it's possible to rise, phoenix-like, from the ashes of personal challenges and to rediscover passion and purpose. Donovan's story, marked by highs and lows, victories and setbacks, mirrors the unpredictable nature of life itself. It's a story that encourages athletes to listen to their hearts and to remember that it's never too late to return to what they love, to face their struggles head-on, and to lead by example, both on and off the pitch.

In this book of soccer tales, each story, including Donovan's, weaves into the broader story of the game's impact on individuals and society. These stories highlight soccer's ability to inspire, unite, and transform. They remind us that the sport is more than just a game; it's a journey filled with lessons on resilience, leadership, and the courage to face personal battles.

As we turn the page, let's carry forward the spirit of perseverance, the importance of mental health awareness, and the enduring influence of leadership. These themes, universal and timeless, set the stage for the next chapter in our exploration of soccer's most epic tales.

21

THE TACTICAL MAESTROS OF ITALY

Imagine standing in the heart of Rome, gazing up at the Colosseum, its ancient structure whispering tales of strategy and conquest. Just as these walls have stood the test of time, so too has Italy's approach to football, a blend of tactical nous and defensive solidity that has fascinated and frustrated in equal measure. This chapter peels back the layers of Italy's defensive artistry, tracing its roots, celebrating its pioneers, and examining its influence on the beautiful game's modern canvas.

In football, Italy's defensive strategy has always been about more than just preventing goals. It's akin to a chess grandmaster foreseeing moves ahead, a meticulous sculptor chiseling away to reveal form and structure. Italian defenses operate on anticipation, understanding, and a collective will to protect their goal as if it were their crown jewel. This approach has seen Italy clinch four World Cups, their teams often outthinking rather than outplaying their opponents. Their 2006 World Cup victory stands as a pinnacle of this strategic mastery, where Italy conceded only two goals throughout the tournament. Their matches weren't just won on the pitch; they were won in the tactical blueprints laid out by their coach, Marcello Lippi, who orchestrated a symphony of defensive resilience.

Catenaccio, Italy's hallmark defensive system, translates to "door bolt," a fitting metaphor for a strategy designed to lock down their half of the pitch. It originated in the 1960s, a brainchild of Helenio Herrera, the then coach of Inter Milan. The system hinges on a robust defense, anchored by a sweeper or libero behind the main defensive line, ready to clean up any breaches. But catenaccio is no relic; it has evolved, blending with more modern, possession-based approaches. Coaches like Antonio Conte and Carlo Ancelotti have folded catenaccio principles into their tactics, creating teams that are as adept at launching swift counter-attacks as they are at shutting down opponents.

Italy's defensive artistry is personified by its legendary defenders, masters of their craft whose names are etched in football's hall of fame. Paolo Maldini and Franco Baresi, both icons of AC Milan and the Italian national team, stand out as paragons of defensive excellence. Maldini, with his grace under pressure, and Baresi, with his tactical intelligence, were not just defenders; they were artists painting clean sheets with every match. Their legacy is a masterclass in defense, inspiring generations to view the role not as a last line of resistance but as a position of influence and control.

Italy's defensive philosophy has left an indelible mark on the tactical landscape of modern football. Teams across the globe, from the Premier League to La Liga, have incorporated aspects of the Italian defensive mindset into their strategies. This influence extends beyond club football, shaping national teams' approaches in major tournaments. The emphasis on a solid defensive foundation, coupled with the capacity to transition quickly into attack, is a formula many strive to replicate. Italy's success on the international stage serves as evidence of the efficacy of their approach, a blueprint that balances defensive rigour with attacking potential.

Italian football's tactical journey mirrors the evolution of the Colosseum itself, from a bastion of defense to a symbol of enduring beauty and strategy. The lessons drawn from Italy's approach extend beyond the pitch, offering insights into the value of preparation, unity, and adaptability. As the modern game continues to evolve, the essence of Italian tactical mastery remains a cornerstone, a reminder that sometimes, the art of defense is the most potent form of attack.

22

GERMANY'S REBIRTH: THE 2014 WORLD CUP STRATEGY

The tale of Germany's football renaissance, culminating in their 2014 World Cup victory, is one of meticulous planning, innovation, and a collective spirit. This epoch marked a departure from traditional approaches, embracing a future where each player's potential could be maximized through a blend of youth development, a high-pressing game, and the insightful use of data analytics.

At the heart of Germany's transformation was a radical overhaul of their tactical philosophy. Post-2000, German football found itself at a crossroads, necessitating a shift towards a more dynamic, technically proficient model. This shift was underpinned by a renewed focus on youth development, emphasizing technical skills, versatility, and mental fortitude. Academies across the nation adopted this ethos, fostering environments where young talents could flourish. The fruits of this labor were evident in players like Thomas Müller and Mesut Özil, who became icons of Germany's fluid, attacking style. Their ability to interchange positions, coupled with superior technical skills, became the cornerstone of Germany's tactical identity, ensuring the team was greater than the sum of its parts.

A pivotal element in Germany's tactical arsenal was the high-pressing game. This strategy, predicated on winning the ball back swiftly after losing possession, was executed with precision against top-tier opponents. The idea was simple yet effective: apply pressure on the opposition's defenders, force errors, and transition quickly from defense to attack. This approach was most memorably deployed against Brazil in the 2014 World Cup semi-final, where Germany's relentless pressing and swift counter-attacks dismantled the host nation. The execution of this strategy required not only physical fitness but also acute spatial awareness and tactical discipline, attributes that the German squad had in abundance.

The adoption of data analytics played a crucial role in optimizing player performance and refining in-game tactics. Germany's coaching staff, led by Joachim Löw, leveraged advanced metrics to gain insights into player fitness, opposition weaknesses, and potential tactical adjustments. This data-driven approach allowed for a level of preparation and adaptability that was previously unattainable. By analyzing patterns and tendencies, Germany could tailor their training, set-pieces, and overall game plan to exploit their opponents' vulnerabilities, a strategy that proved instrumental in their World Cup campaign.

The legacy of Germany's 2014 triumph extends far beyond the trophy and the accolades. It set a new benchmark for national teams worldwide, illustrating the power of systemic youth development, tactical flexibility, and the strategic use of analytics. Future teams, both at the club and international levels, have looked to Germany's model as a blueprint for success. The emphasis on producing technically skilled players who are tactically astute and versatile has become a guiding principle for academies globally. Moreover, the integration of data analytics into the fabric of team preparation and strategy has underscored the importance of innovation in maintaining a competitive edge.

Germany's World Cup victory was a testament to the effectiveness of their strategic overhaul. It underscored the significance of embracing change, fostering talent from the grassroots, and leveraging technology to enhance performance. This holistic approach to football, blending tradition with innovation, not only rejuvenated German football but also offered valuable lessons on the evolution of the modern game.

23

THE DUTCH TOTAL FOOTBALL LEGACY

The Dutch approach to football, widely recognized as Total Football, is akin to a river's nature: constantly moving, adapting its course, but always maintaining its strength and purpose. This philosophy, deeply rooted in the ethos of fluidity, versatility, and collective play, has not just defined a team or a nation but has fundamentally altered the landscape of global football.

Total Football's essence lies in its radical departure from rigid positions and structured play. At its core, it champions the idea that any player can take over the role of any other player in the team. This fluidity allows for a dynamic, unpredictable style of play, emphasizing adaptability and understanding among teammates. This philosophy underpins a belief in the collective over the individual, where the synchrony and interchangeability of players lead to a harmonious and efficient style of play that can dominate and dictate the pace of the game.

The impact of Total Football on the Netherlands' national team and clubs, particularly Ajax, has been profound and enduring. In the 1970s, the world witnessed the emergence of a Dutch side that played with an elegance and intelligence that was, at the time, unparalleled. Ajax, under the guidance of Rinus Michels and the genius of Johan Cruyff, became the standard-bearer of this philosophy, translating it into a series of domestic and European successes. This period saw Ajax secure three consecutive European Cups, a feat that underscored the effectiveness and allure of Total Football. For the national team, the zenith of this philosophy was reached in the 1974 World Cup, where the Netherlands, though they didn't lift the trophy, captivated the footballing world with their style, earning the moniker "The Clockwork Orange" for their precision, movement, and tactical discipline.

Johan Cruyff and Rinus Michels are indelibly linked to the legacy of Total Football, both as architects and as its most fervent practitioners. Michels, the mastermind, introduced the world to a philosophy that challenged conventional wisdom, crafting a team that played with an almost telepathic understanding. Cruyff, the prodigy within this system, was the embodiment of Total Football on the pitch. His intelligence, technical ability, and vision were pivotal, both for Ajax and the national team. Together, Michels and Cruyff not only revolutionized Dutch football but also inspired a generation of players and coaches to think about the game from a new perspective.

The ripples of Total Football have touched every corner of the modern footballing world, influencing tactics, coaching philosophies, and the very way the game is played. Barcelona's tiki-taka style, under the stewardship of Pep Guardiola, is perhaps the most direct descendant of Total Football, emphasizing possession, player movement, and flexibility. Guardiola, an ardent admirer of Cruyff's principles, has successfully adapted and implemented these ideas, achieving remarkable success. Beyond Barcelona, the principles of Total Football have permeated the tactical approaches of teams across Europe and the world, advocating for a style of play that values intelligence, adaptability, and collective excellence over rigid structures and individual stardom.

The legacy of Dutch Total Football is a testament to the power of innovation and the enduring impact of a philosophy that transcends generations. Its principles of fluidity, versatility, and collective play have not just enriched the tactical discourse but have also elevated the aesthetic and intellectual appreciation of the game. As football continues to evolve, the essence of Total Football remains a beacon, guiding the sport towards ever-greater heights of creativity and excellence.

24

FRANCE'S MULTICULTURAL TRIUMPH: 1998 AND 2018 WORLD CUPS

In the sphere of global football, France's glorious campaigns in the 1998 and 2018 FIFA World Cups stand as testaments to the power of diversity and the strategic brilliance that can be harnessed from a blend of cultures and talents. These victories, spaced two decades apart, reflect not just moments of sporting excellence but also milestones in the evolution of French football, both tactically and socially.

The fabric of France's national teams in both victorious years was woven with threads from various backgrounds, cultures, and heritages. This multicultural assembly of players showcased France's demographic diversity, turning it into their strongest asset on the football pitch. The 1998 squad, affectionately dubbed "Les Bleus," showcased talents like Zinedine Zidane of Algerian descent, Lilian Thuram from the Caribbean, and Patrick Vieira, who was born in Senegal. Fast forward to 2018, and the story continued with stars like Kylian Mbappé, whose roots trace back to Cameroon and Algeria, and N'Golo Kanté, of Malian heritage. The fusion of these diverse backgrounds created teams with a broad spectrum of styles, skills, and mentalities, making the French squad unpredictable and adaptable, qualities that proved decisive in their journey to the pinnacle of world football.

The tactical approach employed by France in both tournaments underscored their ability to adapt and evolve in the face of varied opposition. Under the management of Aimé Jacquet in 1998 and Didier Deschamps in 2018, France demonstrated a remarkable tactical flexibility, seamlessly shifting formations and strategies to exploit their opponents' weaknesses while fortifying their own defensive structure. Whether it was adopting a more defensive posture against Brazil in 1998 or unleashing the blistering pace of Mbappé on counter-attacks in 2018, France's tactical acumen was a key driver in their triumphant campaigns. This ability to adjust tactically, coupled with the players' technical proficiency, allowed France to navigate through the tournaments with a blend of flair and solidity.

Leadership played a pivotal role in unifying France's diverse talents into cohesive, winning units. Didier Deschamps, the linchpin of the 1998 team, transitioned into a guiding force as the coach of the 2018 squad, becoming one of the few individuals to win the World Cup both as a player and a coach. His understanding of the pressures of the World Cup, combined with his tactical knowledge, helped in crafting teams that were mentally resilient and strategically astute. Deschamps' leadership extended beyond tactics; his ability to manage egos, expectations, and the media spotlight ensured that the squad remained focused and united in their pursuit of glory.

The ripple effects of France's World Cup victories have been profound, influencing the development of football in the country at every level. These triumphs have propelled football to the forefront of the national consciousness, inspiring a new generation of players across the country. Grassroots initiatives and youth academies have seen increased investment and interest, aiming to replicate the success of their national heroes. Furthermore, the victories have played a critical role in promoting inclusivity and unity, using football as a bridge between diverse communities within France. The multicultural makeup of the victorious squads has sent a powerful message about the strength of diversity, encouraging a more inclusive approach to talent development in football.

In essence, France's World Cup victories in 1998 and 2018 are more than just moments of sporting triumph; they are landmarks in the journey of French football and society. Through a combination of diverse talents, tactical flexibility, inspired leadership, and a profound impact on the nation's footballing culture, these victories encapsulate the essence of what makes football truly the beautiful game.

25

THE EVOLUTION OF GOALKEEPING

The role of the goalkeeper has transformed dramatically from the early days of football, evolving from the traditional shot-stopper to an integral component of team play and strategy. This transformation has not only redefined the position but has also influenced the way teams approach both defense and attack.

Historically, goalkeepers were viewed primarily as the last line of defense, their main task to prevent the ball from crossing the goal line. However, as the game has evolved, so too has the expectation placed on those guarding the net. Modern goalkeepers are now part of the team's offensive play, with their ability to distribute the ball quickly and accurately becoming as valued as their shot-stopping prowess. This shift has seen goalkeepers become a vital part of the team's build-up play, initiating attacks with their distribution and even assisting in controlling the game's tempo.

Technology has played a significant role in enhancing

goalkeeping techniques, from the design of gloves that improve grip and protection to the use of video analysis in training. Training methods have also seen a technological overhaul, with simulators and VR being used to replicate match scenarios, allowing goalkeepers to practice their reactions to a variety of shots and game situations without the physical strain of repeated live drills.

The journey of the goalkeeper's evolution is marked by individuals who have redefined what it means to play between the sticks. Gianluigi Buffon, with his career spanning over two decades, has set the standard for longevity and consistency, combining traditional shot-stopping skills with modern requirements of playmaking and ball distribution. Manuel Neuer, often credited with popularizing the "sweeper-keeper" role, has taken the concept of a goalkeeper to new heights. Neuer's ability to read the game, coupled with his exceptional skills with the ball at his feet, has made him a blueprint for the modern goalkeeper.

Looking ahead, the evolution of goalkeeping is set to continue, with an increasing emphasis on footwork, distribution, and even goal-scoring capabilities. The training of future goalkeepers will likely focus more on these areas, integrating them as key components of a goalkeeper's skill set. Additionally, technological advancements, both in equipment and training methodologies, will further refine the precision and effectiveness of goalkeepers. The integration of data analytics into training and game preparation will provide goalkeepers with insights into opponent strategies, enhancing their ability to anticipate and react to threats.

The transformation of the goalkeeping role reflects

the broader evolution of football itself, a game that continues to adapt and innovate. Goalkeepers, once the last line of defense, are now pivotal to the way teams approach their game, a trend that promises to make the position even more dynamic and influential in the future.

26

THE SOUTH AMERICAN FLAIR: DRIBBLING THROUGH HISTORY

In the vibrant streets of South America, where the rhythm of samba blends with the echoes of bustling markets, lies the cradle of football's most mesmerizing dribblers. This region's unique flair for dribbling isn't merely a product of individual brilliance but a reflection of its rich cultural history and the spontaneous, creative essence of street football. Here, the game is not just a sport; it's an expression of joy, identity, and freedom.

The roots of South America's enchanting dribbling style are deeply embedded in its street football culture. In the narrow alleys and makeshift pitches, where space is a luxury, players learn to navigate tight corners with deft touches and audacious maneuvers. This environment, where creativity thrives and the game flows with an unrestrained spirit, fosters a distinctive style of play characterized by flair, improvisation, and a boldness to take on opponents one-on-one. This style mirrors the region's broader cultural ethos, celebrating individual expression within a collective rhythm, much like the dance of samba that syncs individual flair with communal harmony.

The pantheon of South American football is adorned with names that have transcended the sport, becoming symbols of the region's dribbling heritage. Diego Maradona and Ronaldinho stand as titans, their legacies woven with moments of sublime skill that have captivated fans around the globe. Maradona's 'Hand of God' might headline his legend, but it's his slaloming run against England in the same game in the 1986 World Cup, weaving through defenders with balletic grace, that encapsulates his genius. Ronaldinho, with his infectious smile, brought a playful audacity to the pitch, his feet scripting poetry in motion, most notably in a game where his standing ovation from Real Madrid fans, a rare homage from rivals, underscored the universal admiration for his talent.

The integration of this dribbling flair into tactical setups is a hallmark of South American teams, who balance individual creativity with strategic team play. Coaches from this region often build their tactics around the unique skills of their dribblers, creating systems that allow for moments of individual brilliance without sacrificing the team's overall cohesion. This approach is evident in teams like Brazil's 2002 World Cup squad, where the freedom given to Ronaldo, Rivaldo, and Ronaldinho to express themselves led to a display of football that was as effective as it was enchanting. The tactical frameworks employed by South American teams don't just accommodate dribbling; they celebrate it, understanding that these moments of creativity can unlock defenses and change the course of games.

In an era where football has become increasingly structured and data-driven, the question of how South American flair is being preserved and evolved is poignant.

Despite the global trend towards tactical rigidity, South American teams continue to nurture dribblers, recognizing them as bearers of the region's footballing identity. Youth academies emphasize skill development, encouraging young players to develop their dribbling abilities and creative thinking on the field. Moreover, modern coaches from the region are finding innovative ways to blend traditional dribbling skills with contemporary tactical demands, ensuring that the essence of South American flair not only survives but thrives in the modern game.

The history of South American football, with its rich hues of skill, creativity, and tactical ingenuity, continues to be a vibrant part of the global football landscape. The region's flair for dribbling, rooted in its cultural and historical ethos, remains a testament to the enduring beauty and spirit of the game. As football marches forward, the dribbling artistry of South America dances on, a reminder of the sport's capacity to enchant, inspire, and evolve.

27

SPAIN'S TIKI-TAKA: DOMINANCE THROUGH POSSESSION

In the lush fields of Spain, a revolution quietly took root, one that would redefine the boundaries of football with a mesmerizing dance of passes. This revolution was named Tiki-Taka, a term that echoes the sound of a ball being passed rapidly between players. At its heart, Tiki-Taka is more than a tactic; it's a philosophy that champions control through relentless possession, precision in short passing, and perpetual movement, creating a symphony on the pitch that captivates and dominates.

The golden era of Spanish football, marked by their triumphs in the 2010 World Cup and Euro 2012, stands as a testament to Tiki-Taka's effectiveness. During this period, Spain didn't just win; they enchanted, turning each match into a display of tactical superiority and artistic expression. Their dominance was not enforced through sheer physicality but through a ballet of passes that often left opponents chasing shadows, a testament to a system that prized the ball as the most precious asset on the pitch.

The architects behind this captivating style were influential coaches who saw the game not just as a competition but as an art form. Pep Guardiola, during his tenure at Barcelona, and Vicente del Bosque, at the helm of the national team, were pivotal in championing Tiki-Taka. Guardiola's Barcelona mesmerized the world, transforming the club into the epitome of this philosophy, with players like Xavi Hernandez, Andres Iniesta, and Lionel Messi becoming the custodians of Tiki-Taka. Del Bosque, on the other hand, seamlessly translated this club-level success to the national team, crafting a squad that was unbeatable at its peak, a team that moved and thought as one.

However, the path of Tiki-Taka has not been without its hurdles. As defensive tactics evolved, teams began devising methods to counter Spain's possession-heavy approach. The reliance on maintaining possession sometimes led to predictability, with opponents setting up deep, compact defenses designed to frustrate and force errors. This challenge prompted adaptations, with coaches introducing variations to inject more directness and unpredictability into the play. Such adaptations ensured that Tiki-Taka remained a potent force, capable of evolving in the face of tactical innovations aimed at nullifying its effectiveness.

Tiki-Taka's influence on the game has been profound, altering how teams and coaches across the world view possession and movement. Its principles have permeated various levels of football, from grassroots academies to top-tier clubs, advocating for a style of play that values intelligence and teamwork over brute force. This legacy of Tiki-Taka, with its emphasis on possession, short passing, and movement, continues to inspire a new generation of players and coaches, a tribute to a philosophy that has left an indelible mark on the beautiful game.

28

THE CELTIC TIGERS: IRELAND'S 1990 WORLD CUP JOURNEY

In 1990, a small island nation on the westernmost edge of Europe dared to dream. Ireland, not traditionally known for footballing prowess on the global stage, embarked on a World Cup adventure that would immortalize their names into the history books of the sport. This was a team that thrived under the label of underdogs, a squad that personified resilience and an unyielding spirit that captured the imagination of fans worldwide.

At its core, Ireland's campaign was fueled by an underdog spirit that resonated deeply with the footballing world. Each match was a testament to their tenacity, a showcase of a team refusing to bow down to the giants of the game. This spirit was not born in the locker room talks or the tactical boards; it was woven into the fabric of the team's identity, a reflection of a nation's character that prides itself on fighting against the odds. The world watched in awe as Ireland, with their backs against the wall, stood tall against opponents who underestimated the heart of the Celtic Tigers.

The architect of this remarkable journey was none other than Jack Charlton. A World Cup winner with England in 1966, Charlton brought to Ireland a wealth of experience and a tactical acumen that transformed the team. His influence extended beyond formations and strategies; Charlton instilled in his squad a belief in themselves and their capabilities. Under his guidance, Ireland adopted a style of play that was direct and effective, leveraging their strengths and nullifying the threats posed by more technically gifted teams. Charlton's man-management skills fostered a camaraderie that became Ireland's greatest weapon, turning the team into a close-knit unit ready to battle for every inch on the pitch.

The group stage clash against England, a gritty affair that ended in a draw, set the tone for Ireland's campaign, signaling their intent and resilience. However, it was the match against Romania that remains etched in the hearts of the Irish faithful. A nerve-wracking encounter that went to penalties saw Ireland emerge victorious, securing a place in the quarter-finals, a feat that was beyond the wildest dreams of many supporters. Each game was a chapter in a fairy tale that saw Ireland, a team of modest expectations, daring to dream big. They unfortunately lost the quarter-final to hosts Italy, but their mark on the soccer sphere was there for the world to see.

The impact of Ireland's 1990 World Cup journey reverberates to this day, a legacy that transcends the realm of football. It was a moment that united the nation, instilling a sense of pride and belief in the hearts of millions. For young fans watching, it was an introduction to the joy and heartache of football, igniting passions that would see a new generation dream of wearing the green jersey. The legacy of the 1990 squad has been a guiding light for Irish football, a beacon that reminds us that with heart, unity, and a bit of luck, anything is possible.

The influence of this historic campaign has been profound, shaping the development of the sport in Ireland. Grassroots initiatives saw a surge in participation, with children across the nation inspired by the exploits of their heroes. The success of the national team also had a tangible impact on the domestic league, raising the profile of football in a country where Gaelic sports traditionally dominated. This World Cup adventure inspired a renaissance in Irish football, fostering a culture that values perseverance, teamwork, and the audacious belief that underdogs can have their day.

The story of Ireland's 1990 World Cup odyssey is a testament to the beauty of football, a sport that thrives on the unexpected, celebrates the underdog, and brings together a nation. It's a story that reminds us of the power of sport to inspire, unite, and leave a lasting impact on the hearts and minds of fans and players alike. Ireland's journey in Italy was more than a series of football matches; it was a moment in time that captured the essence of the beautiful game, a reminder that on the world's biggest stage, dreams can come true.

29

THE RISE OF FOOTBALL ACADEMIES: LA MASIA AND BEYOND

In the heart of Catalonia, nestled within the bustling city of Barcelona, lies La Masia, an academy whose name resonates far beyond its physical bounds. This isn't merely a training facility; it's a crucible where the raw ore of potential is refined into the gold of footballing mastery. La Masia, alongside other renowned academies, stands at the forefront of a movement that has reshaped the landscape of football, emphasizing not just the development of players but the cultivation of a philosophy that intertwines with the very identity of the clubs they represent.

At La Masia, the focus transcends the mere honing of physical skills. Here, the game is taught as a language, with emphasis on communication through passes, movement as dialogue, and possession as a form of expression. This philosophy, deeply embedded in the teachings of Johan Cruyff and furthered by visionaries like Pep Guardiola, prioritizes intelligence, creativity, and a profound understanding of space and timing. Training sessions are meticulously designed to instill these principles from an early age, crafting players capable of interpreting the game in ways that elevate their play from mere action to art. This approach has been mirrored by academies worldwide, with each adapting the core premise to their cultural and tactical context, fostering environments where young talents are encouraged to think, adapt, and innovate.

The proof of La Masia's success lies in the stars it has produced, players whose names have become synonymous with excellence in football. From Lionel Messi, whose wizardry on the ball is unparalleled, to Xavi Hernandez and Andres Iniesta, maestros of midfield orchestration, the academy has consistently produced talents who have not only succeeded at the club level but have also left indelible marks on the international stage. This model of development has served as an inspiration for clubs across the globe, leading to the establishment of academies that aspire to replicate the success of La Masia. The impact of these institutions is profound, providing a pipeline of talent that sustains clubs and national teams alike, ensuring a steady influx of players who carry forward the philosophies and ideals ingrained in them during their formative years.

Despite the undeniable successes, football academies face their share of challenges and criticisms. The pressure exerted on young prospects can be immense, with the weight of expectations often leading to burnout and disillusionment. This intense focus on development and performance, while aimed at nurturing talent, can sometimes overshadow the need for a balanced life, placing undue stress on individuals still navigating their formative years. Furthermore, the commercialization of youth development has raised concerns, with academies at times being seen as factories churning out talent in pursuit of profit rather than centers of learning and growth. Balancing the commercial aspects with the developmental and educational needs of young players remains a delicate task, requiring a nuanced approach that prioritizes the well-being and holistic development of the individuals under their care.

The ripple effect of successful academies like La Masia is felt worldwide, inspiring the creation of similar institutions that seek to emulate their philosophy and success. From the cobblestone streets of Amsterdam to the vibrant landscapes of São Paulo, academies have become beacons of hope and hubs of talent, each contributing to the global history of football. The cross-pollination of ideas and methodologies has enriched the sport, fostering a diverse ecosystem where talents from varying backgrounds and cultures converge, elevating the level of play and competition across continents. This global network of academies not only ensures a vibrant future for football but also reinforces the sport's power to unite, inspire, and transform lives, transcending geographical, cultural, and social divides.

As the sun sets over La Masia, casting long shadows across the training fields, it's clear that the legacy of football academies is not just in the stars they produce but in the dreams they nurture. These institutions stand as custodians of the game's future, guardians of a heritage that they continue to enrich with each passing generation.

30

THE PSYCHOLOGY OF PENALTY SHOOTOUTS

In the high-stakes drama of football, few moments grip the heart like a penalty shootout. Standing twelve yards from goal, a player faces not just the opposing goalkeeper but a barrage of internal pressures, a test of nerve and skill distilled into a single kick. This segment peels back the layers of mental and strategic preparation that underpin these nail-biting finales, shining a light on the psychological duel at the heart of every penalty shootout.

The mental labyrinth that players navigate during a penalty shootout is complex. Techniques for mental fortitude in these moments vary, from visualization exercises to controlled breathing routines, aiming to steady the nerves and maintain focus. Players often rehearse this scenario in their minds, picturing the ball hitting the back of the net, a practice that bolsters confidence and combats the paralysis of overthinking. Some embrace routines or superstitions that have accompanied personal successes, lending an air of familiarity and control in an otherwise pressure-laden situation.

On the flip side, goalkeepers face their own psychological and strategic battle in anticipating the kicker's move. Some delve into comprehensive studies of their opponents' penalty habits, looking for patterns or tells that might give away the intended direction of the shot. Others employ gamesmanship, seeking to disrupt the kicker's focus with movement on the line or verbal exchanges. The moment before a penalty is a mind game, where goalkeepers balance instinct with insight, often deciding their actions in the split second of the run-up, a testament to the blend of preparation and spontaneity that defines this role.

The football history books are rich with shootouts that have turned players into legends and moments into folklore. The 1994 World Cup final saw Brazil clinch the title in a shootout against Italy, with Roberto Baggio's missed penalty casting a long shadow over his illustrious career. Conversely, the 2005 Champions League final showcased Jerzy Dudek's heroics for Liverpool, employing a wobbly-legged technique inspired by Bruce Grobbelaar to clinch victory. These moments, ingrained in the memories of fans, underscore the thin line between agony and ecstasy that defines penalty shootouts.

The realm of science offers intriguing insights into the psychology of penalty shootouts. Studies have explored various aspects, from the advantage of shooting first, linked to higher success rates, to the goalkeeper's dive direction, with tendencies showing a preference for their right. Researchers have also delved into the kicker's decision-making process, highlighting the split-second interplay between instinct and strategy. These studies not only enrich our understanding of the shootout but also offer teams and players data-driven strategies to enhance their preparation and performance in these crucible moments.

In football, the penalty shootout stands as a testament to the game's capacity to enthrall, to challenge, and to leave a mark on the hearts and minds of those who witness it. From the meticulous preparation of players and goalkeepers to the historical showdowns that have defined careers and tournaments, shootouts encapsulate the essence of football's drama. It's the pinnacle of excitement for a neutral or winning fan, but for the losing side, penalities signify an event they'd like to forget for the rest of their lives.

31

TECHNOLOGY IN FOOTBALL: VAR AND BEYOND

The advent of Video Assistant Referees (VAR) in football marked a pivotal moment in the sport's history, a step towards minimizing human error and ensuring fairness in the heat of competition. At its core, VAR was introduced to aid on-field referees in making more accurate decisions regarding goals, penalties, direct red card incidents, and mistaken identity. Yet, this innovation has not been without its controversies, stirring debates on the essence of the game, the flow of play, and the spirit of spontaneity that football embodies.

VAR's primary objective is to bring clarity and fairness to critical decisions. However, its application has sparked discussions, with critics arguing it disrupts the game's natural rhythm and places undue stress on referees. Supporters counter that by highlighting its role in correcting clear and obvious errors, thus enhancing the sport's integrity.

The landscape of football technology extends well beyond VAR, encompassing advancements that have transformed aspects of training, strategy, and player performance evaluation.

Goal-Line Technology: This system provides instantaneous feedback on whether the ball has crossed the goal line, offering a definitive answer to one of the game's most contentious questions. Its accuracy and speed have made it an indispensable tool in modern football.

Performance Tracking Systems: Wearable tech and advanced analytics platforms now track every run, pass, and tackle, offering insights into player performance, fitness levels, and risk of injury. These systems allow coaches to tailor training regimes and match strategies to the unique profiles of their teams and opponents.

The impact of technology on football is multifaceted, influencing not only how decisions are made on the pitch but also how teams prepare for matches and how players develop and maintain peak condition.

Referee Decisions: The introduction of VAR has led to more accurate calls on pivotal moments, albeit at the cost of pacing and spontaneous celebration. This trade-off continues to fuel debates on technology's place in the sport.

Tactics: The wealth of data available through performance tracking has led to more nuanced tactical approaches. Coaches now make decisions based on comprehensive analytics, leading to strategies that are increasingly tailored and sophisticated.

Player Performance Analysis: The detailed analysis provided by tracking systems enables a deeper understanding of player strengths, weaknesses, and areas for development. This personalized insight helps in optimizing training and recovery, pushing the boundaries of individual and team performance.

Looking to the future, technological innovations promise to further reshape football, opening new horizons for the sport's evolution.

Augmented and Virtual Reality: AR and VR technologies hold the potential to revolutionize training and fan experiences. Players could train in simulated environments that mimic match conditions without the physical strain, while fans might enjoy immersive viewing experiences that bring them closer to the action.

Artificial Intelligence in Tactics and Scouting: AI could further refine the process of scouting and tactical analysis, predicting opponent strategies and identifying emerging talents with unprecedented precision.

Biometric Monitoring: Advancements in biometric technology could offer real-time insights into players' physiological states, allowing for immediate adjustments in training and during matches to optimize performance and prevent injuries.

These prospective developments hint at a future where the integration of technology in football is even more seamless and impactful, enhancing the sport's integrity, safety, and engagement for players, coaches, and fans alike. The journey of technology in football, from VAR to the horizons of AI and biometrics, reflects a broader story of progress and adaptation, a testament to the sport's enduring quest for excellence and fairness.

32

THE UNSEEN HEROES: FOOTBALL SCOUTS

In the realm of football, where the bright lights often shine on the players and the tactical geniuses orchestrating from the sidelines, there exists a group of pivotal figures operating away from the limelight. These are the scouts, the unsung heroes whose keen eyes and deep understanding of the game play a critical role in shaping the future of clubs and national teams. Their work, though less visible, is the foundation upon which teams are built and successes are forged.

Scouts are the bridge between raw talent and professional football, identifying players who not only possess exceptional skills but also fit the tactical and cultural ethos of the team they represent. Their expertise lies not just in recognizing current ability but in foreseeing a player's potential to develop, adapt, and thrive at the highest levels of the game.

The journey of scouting has witnessed a significant transformation, evolving from a reliance on personal networks and chance sightings to a sophisticated blend of traditional observation and cutting-edge technology.

Initially, scouting was heavily dependent on personal contacts and extensive travel, with scouts frequenting local games in search of the next big talent. This method, while effective, was limited by the scouts' geographical reach and the sheer unpredictability of stumbling upon a future star. The digital age has revolutionized scouting, introducing tools that allow scouts to assess players from across the globe without leaving their desks. Data analytics provide insights into a player's performance metrics, while video analysis enables a detailed examination of a player's technique, decision-making, and adaptability in various situations. This blend of traditional scouting with technology has expanded the scope of talent identification, making it a more precise and efficient process.

Several stories of famous players discovered by scouts highlight the critical eye and foresight that scouting requires. Jamie Vardy was one of these players. From playing in the lower leagues to becoming a Premier League champion with Leicester City, Vardy's journey is a testament to the scouts who saw his potential and the impact he could make at the highest level. Arguably the biggest 'catch' a scout has made is when Horacio Gaggioli found Lionel Messi and took him to Barcelona. Signed by the Spanish club at a young age, Messi's transition from a talented youngster in Argentina to a global icon underscores the scouts' role in identifying and nurturing generational talent.

Looking into the future, scouting faces both challenges and opportunities, particularly with the continuous advancements in technology. Technological Advancements: The increasing reliance on data and analytics poses a challenge to balance the quantitative aspects of scouting with the qualitative insights gained from personal observation. However, it also presents an opportunity to refine scouting processes, making them more comprehensive and accurate. Expanding Global Reach: Technology enables scouts to discover talent in previously untapped regions, broadening the diversity and richness of football talent. This global reach challenges scouts to understand a wider array of football cultures and playing styles, enriching the scouting process and the game itself.

As the scouting process becomes more intrusive, with players as young as eight or nine coming under scrutiny, the football community faces ethical questions about the pressure and expectations placed on young talents. Balancing ambition with the well-being of prospective players will be a critical consideration for the future of scouting.

The evolution of scouting in football mirrors the game's own growth and transformation. From humble beginnings to a sophisticated, technology-driven process, scouting remains at the heart of football's future, continually seeking out the stars of tomorrow. The scouts, with their unique blend of insight, experience, and an unerring eye for talent, are the true architects of football's future, crafting teams and shaping legends away from the roar of the crowds but at the very core of the beautiful game's enduring allure.

33

THE MIRACLE OF BERN: GERMANY'S 1954 WORLD CUP

Imagine standing in a packed stadium, the crowd's roar echoing like thunder, each fan's heart syncing with the rhythm of the game. This isn't just about watching football; it's about experiencing it, living every high and low alongside thousands of others. It's in these bustling arenas that the true essence of football reveals itself—not just as a game played on the pitch but as a shared experience that unites people across the globe. This chapter dives into the world of football fandom, exploring the moments and movements that have shaped the culture of support around this beautiful game.

In 1954, a nation found hope on the football pitch. Germany's victory in the World Cup wasn't just about lifting a trophy; it was about lifting the spirits of a country trying to rebuild after the devastation of war. Let's break down how this underdog win became a cornerstone for German football fans and the nation as a whole.

On a rainy afternoon in Bern, Switzerland, the German national team, facing the mighty Hungarians, pulled off one of the most unexpected victories in World

Cup history. Hungary came into the final unbeaten and favored to win, but Germany's 3-2 triumph was a David versus Goliath tale that resonated far beyond the football field. It was a moment of sheer disbelief, turning into uncontrollable joy for German fans and citizens alike. This win provided a much-needed morale boost, showing a war-ravaged country that recovery and success were possible.

The win sparked a football fever across Germany, igniting a passion for the game that has endured for decades. Suddenly, football became more than just a pastime; it was a source of pride and unity. Fans across the country felt a renewed sense of belonging and togetherness, rallying behind their national team as symbols of hope and resilience. The victory in Bern laid the foundation for a fan culture that is today known for its fervent support and loyalty.

The long-term impact of this match on German football and its fans cannot be overstated. It marked the beginning of Germany's ascent to the top of world football, inspiring generations of players and supporters. The "Spirit of Bern" is often evoked as a rallying cry when the odds are stacked against the German team, embodying the belief that anything is possible with determination and unity.

Images from the final—of captain Fritz Walter leading his team in the rain, of Helmut Rahn scoring the winning goal, and of the team lifting the Jules Rimet Trophy—are etched into the collective memory of football fans worldwide. These moments are replayed and recounted, a reminder of the match's significance and its enduring legacy in the hearts of fans.

Football, at its core, is about moments like these—

where underdogs emerge victorious, where fans find a shared identity, and where the beautiful game becomes a beacon of hope and unity. The Miracle of Bern is a testament to football's power to inspire, to unite, and to heal, a story that continues to resonate with fans not just in Germany but around the world.

As we move beyond the Miracle of Bern, our journey through the heartbeat of the stands takes us to different corners of the globe, exploring rivalries, tragedies, and triumphs that have defined football fan culture. Each story, unique in its context and impact, shares a common thread—the profound connection between the game, the players, and the fans who support them through thick and thin.

34

THE PASSION OF BUENOS AIRES: BOCA JUNIORS VS. RIVER PLATE

The air in Buenos Aires carries a charge whenever Boca Juniors and River Plate face off. This isn't just a football match; it's a showdown that stops the city, dividing it along lines of fierce loyalty and passion. This section peels back the layers of the Superclásico, exploring the roots and ramifications of this historic rivalry.

The origin story of Boca Juniors and River Plate is steeped in the working-class neighborhoods of Buenos Aires. Boca, representing the gritty dockside area of La Boca, and River, originally from the same district before moving to the more affluent Núñez, encapsulate a divide that is as much about social class as it is about football. This rivalry, which began in the early 20th century, has grown to become one of the most intense in the sport, fueled by a century of competitive encounters, dramatic matches, and contrasting identities. Each clash is a battle for supremacy, not just in Buenos Aires but in Argentine football.

The Superclásico transcends the boundaries of a mere

football game, embedding itself into the cultural fabric of Buenos Aires and, by extension, Argentina. It's a spectacle that highlights the city's vibrant culture, its passion for football, and its deep-seated traditions. The rivalry is a lens through which the social dynamics and historical tensions within Buenos Aires are magnified, offering insights into the city's identity. On match days, the city transforms, with neighborhoods draped in the colors of their allegiance, showcasing the deep cultural roots and significance of this rivalry.

The fans of Boca Juniors and River Plate are notorious for their fervent support, which manifests in electrifying atmospheres that are unparalleled in football. The stadiums turn into cauldrons of noise, color, and emotion during the Superclásico. Elaborate tifos cover entire stands, choreographed chants resonate, and flares light up the sky, creating a spectacle that's as much for the fans as it is for the players on the pitch. This fanatic support is a testament to the deep connection the clubs have with their communities, showcasing the unwavering loyalty and passion that define Argentine football fandom.

Over the decades, Boca Juniors and River Plate have provided some of the most unforgettable moments in football. Matches that have seen last-minute winners, dramatic comebacks, and controversial decisions add chapters to the lore of the Superclásico. One such encounter, the 2018 Copa Libertadores final, which for the first time in history saw the two rivals face off in the final of South America's premier club competition, had to be played in Madrid due to security concerns. This match, which River Plate won 3-1, was not just a victory on the field but a demonstration of the global reach and intense passion that characterize this rivalry. Each game is a story, each moment a memory etched in the hearts of fans, contributing to the legend of the Superclásico.

The Boca Juniors vs. River Plate rivalry is more than just a football match; it's a phenomenon that captures the essence of passion, loyalty, and identity in sports. Through its historic roots, cultural significance, fanatic support, and memorable clashes, the Superclásico remains one of the most compelling stories in football, a testament to the game's power to captivate and unite.

35

THE GREEN BRIGADE: CELTIC'S VOCAL SUPPORT

In the heart of Glasgow stands Celtic Park, a fortress steeped in history and tradition, where the Green Brigade has emerged as a vocal and visual force. This group of supporters, united under the Celtic banner, has become synonymous with their unwavering support, pushing the boundaries of fandom in football. Their formation and ethos are deeply rooted in Celtic's rich Irish heritage, a connection that has inspired their activism and shaped their identity within the footballing world.

The Green Brigade's inception was driven by a desire to create a more vibrant and supportive atmosphere at Celtic Park, but their purpose quickly expanded. They've woven Celtic's Irish identity and their stance on social causes into the fabric of their support, making statements on issues ranging from political freedom to social justice. This alignment with Celtic's historical roots and the broader social conscience has set them apart, turning the stands into a platform for voicing collective beliefs and values. Their identity is a blend of fierce loyalty to Celtic and a commitment to the causes they champion, epitomizing the power of sports as a catalyst for social change.

Match days at Celtic Park are transformed into spectacles of color and sound, thanks in large part to the Green Brigade. Their meticulously planned tifo displays, ranging from tributes to Celtic legends to messages of social and political relevance, are sights to behold. These visual feats, combined with their relentless singing and chanting, create an electrifying atmosphere that resonates beyond the stadium. The group's creativity and coordination in these displays not only bolster Celtic's home advantage but also bring to life the passion and history of the club, making each match an unforgettable experience.

Beyond the terraces, the Green Brigade's influence extends into the community through their involvement in charitable activities. From organizing food drives to supporting local and international causes, their commitment to making a positive impact is evident. This engagement highlights the group's understanding of their role in the broader community, leveraging their platform and visibility to support those in need. Their actions serve as a reminder of the potential for fan groups to contribute meaningfully to their communities, reinforcing the ties between the club, its supporters, and the wider society.

The path of the Green Brigade has not been without its hurdles. Their outspoken nature and the political undertones of some of their displays have led to clashes with authorities, including the police and Celtic's own management. These incidents have sparked debates over the place of politics in football and the limits of fan expression. Despite these challenges, the group has remained steadfast in its beliefs, often using controversy as a means to further highlight the issues they stand for.

Their resilience in the face of criticism and sanctions has only solidified their standing within the Celtic fanbase, embodying the spirit of defiance and independence that characterizes the club's history.

The Green Brigade's story is a vivid illustration of modern football fandom, where support for the team intertwines with a deeper sense of identity and purpose. Their presence at Celtic Park goes beyond cheering for goals; it's a celebration of Celtic's heritage, a call to action on social issues, and a demonstration of the profound impact supporters can have on their club and community. In the Green Brigade, Celtic has not just a group of fans but a movement, a testament to the enduring power of football to unite and inspire.

36

THE YELLOW WALL: BORUSSIA DORTMUND'S 12TH MAN

In the pulsating heart of Dortmund, Germany, lies a spectacle that embodies the spirit of football like no other—the Yellow Wall. This term, affectionately coined for the South Stand at Signal Iduna Park, isn't just a description of the vivid sea of fans clad in yellow and black. It represents one of the most passionate and unified supporter bases in the world, a force that has become synonymous with Borussia Dortmund's identity and success on the pitch.

The Yellow Wall, with its capacity to host nearly 25,000 standing fans, is a sight to behold. On match days, this towering stand becomes a living, breathing entity, pulsating with energy and noise. The sheer volume and fervor of the crowd create an atmosphere that can intimidate visiting teams while galvanizing Dortmund players. It's this electric environment that has contributed to Signal Iduna Park being dubbed a fortress, where the team's performance is elevated by the unwavering support from the stands. The presence of the Yellow Wall transforms the stadium into more than just a venue for football; it becomes a battleground where Dortmund rarely fails to rise to the occasion.

The culture that thrives within the Yellow Wall is unique, characterized by an unparalleled commitment to the team. This isn't just fandom; it's a way of life for many. The traditions, songs, and rituals that unfold in the South Stand are passed down through generations, creating a bond that transcends the game itself. Fans arrive hours before kick-off, flags and banners in hand, ready to sing their hearts out from the moment the players step onto the pitch until long after the final whistle. This collective expression of support is a testament to the deep connection between the club and its fans, a relationship built on mutual respect and loyalty.

The Yellow Wall has transcended its local origins to become a global phenomenon, attracting football enthusiasts from around the world eager to experience its legendary atmosphere. Visitors flock to Dortmund not just for the football but to be part of something bigger, to stand in the Yellow Wall and feel its power firsthand. This has not only elevated the profile of Borussia Dortmund internationally but has also fostered a sense of pride within the city, showcasing the impact a passionate fan base can have in drawing global attention and admiration.

Time and again, the Yellow Wall has proven to be more than just a backdrop to Dortmund's home games; it has been a decisive factor in the outcome of matches. There are countless instances where the roar of the Wall has spurred the team to victory in the dying minutes of a game, turning seeming defeat into triumphant wins. It's this ability to influence the flow and outcome of matches that truly sets the Yellow Wall apart, embodying the essence of the 12th man on the pitch. Whether rallying behind the team to mount a comeback or defending a slender lead, the impact of the Yellow Wall is felt by players, coaches, and opponents alike.

In Dortmund, football is not just played on the pitch; it's lived in the stands, especially in the Yellow Wall. This massive, heaving mass of yellow and black is more than a section of a stadium—it's the beating heart of Borussia Dortmund, a symbol of unity, passion, and unyielding support. The Wall's influence stretches from the terraces into the fabric of the game, proving time and again that fans are not just spectators; they are an integral part of the team's success. As Dortmund continues to compete at the highest levels, the Yellow Wall remains a steadfast ally, a reminder of the power of collective passion in the beautiful game.

37

THE IBROX DISASTER: TRAGEDY AND TRIUMPH OF HUMAN SPIRIT

In the football history books, certain dates are marked not for the joy or the triumphs they brought, but for the lessons they taught us, the lives they changed, and the marks they left on the heart of the sport. The Ibrox disaster of January 2, 1971, stands as one of those somber moments—a tragedy that unfolded in the closing minutes of an Old Firm match between Rangers and Celtic at Ibrox Stadium in Glasgow, Scotland, claiming 66 lives and leaving over 200 injured. In the aftermath of a match that should have been remembered for the sport, it became a catalyst for change and a poignant reminder of the fragility of life.

On that fateful day, as fans were making their way out of the stadium, a crush occurred on Stairway 13, a notorious exit known for its steep and narrow design. Initial reports suggested that the crush was triggered by fans attempting to return to the stands after hearing a late equalizer, leading to a catastrophic collapse. The immediate aftermath was chaos, with fans and emergency services scrambling to help those caught in the crush. The tragedy deeply affected the victims' families and the wider football community, prompting an outpouring of grief and solidarity across the sport.

The Ibrox disaster became a turning point in the history of football stadium safety. In its wake, significant reforms were implemented to ensure that such a tragedy would never occur again, including the introduction of all-seater stadiums, significantly reducing the chances of such accidents. Additionally, there was a push for better-designed exits and entrances, improved crowd management practices, and more robust safety regulations at football grounds across the UK and beyond. These changes reshaped the way fans experience football, prioritizing their safety and ensuring that the joy of the game is never marred by tragedy.

In the days and weeks following the disaster, a remarkable sense of unity and support emerged within the football community. Fans of Rangers, Celtic, and clubs across Scotland and further afield came together to mourn the loss of life. This collective grieving process showcased the solidarity and compassion inherent within the football family—a reminder that, despite rivalries on the pitch, the community stands as one in times of hardship. Fundraisers and support networks sprang up, providing financial and emotional support to the families affected, a testament to the power of collective action in the face of tragedy.

Today, the legacy of the Ibrox disaster is kept alive through annual remembrance ceremonies and the continued efforts to ensure the safety of all who attend football matches. At Ibrox Stadium, a memorial stands as a poignant reminder of those who lost their lives, ensuring that their memory is honored and the lessons learned from that day are never forgotten. The disaster has fostered a culture of safety in sports, reminding us of the importance of vigilance and care in the management of football events. It has also united fans in a shared commitment to remember and honor those affected, ensuring that the spirit of unity and support forged in the aftermath of the tragedy continues to define the football community.

The Ibrox disaster, while a moment of profound sadness and loss, has also been a story of human resilience, of a community coming together to support those in need, and of a sport that learned and grew stronger in the face of adversity. It serves as a powerful reminder of the importance of safety, the value of human life, and the unbreakable spirit of the football community.

38

THE TRAGEDY AND TRIUMPH OF HILLSBOROUGH

There's another event in British football history that shocked the world as much as the Ibrox disaster.

On a spring afternoon in 1989, the world of football was changed forever by a harrowing event at Hillsborough Stadium in Sheffield, England. This disaster unfolded during the FA Cup semi-final match between Liverpool and Nottingham Forest, marking one of the darkest days in the history of the sport. What began as a day of high spirits and anticipation turned into chaos and tragedy, deeply affecting the families of the victims, the survivors, and the broader football community.

The disaster's immediate aftermath was a scene of unimaginable sorrow and confusion. Ninety-seven Liverpool fans lost their lives because of a crush in the Leppings Lane end of the stadium, with hundreds more injured. The pain of the families and friends of those who perished was unimaginable, their grief compounded by initial misinformation and blame wrongly placed on the victims. The football community, both in the UK and around the world, was united in mourning, with tributes pouring in and matches paused to honor those who had lost their lives.

The aftermath of the Hillsborough disaster saw the bereaved families embark on a long and arduous journey for justice, challenging initial stories that unfairly blamed the fans for the tragedy. Supported by the global football community, their relentless pursuit of truth led to the Hillsborough Independent Panel's formation, which, after examining previously undisclosed documents, cleared the fans of any wrongdoing. This fight for justice, spanning decades, highlighted the resilience and determination of the families and the wider community to ensure that those lost were remembered rightly and that such a tragedy would never happen again.

In response to the Hillsborough disaster, significant changes were implemented in stadium designs and safety regulations, transforming how football matches are viewed and attended. The Taylor Report, commissioned in the immediate aftermath, led to the recommendation that all major stadiums convert to an all-seater model, drastically improving crowd control and reducing the likelihood of similar disasters. Other safety measures introduced included more rigorous standards for stadium certification, improved access and egress routes, and enhanced monitoring and management of crowd densities. These reforms have made football stadiums safer for fans, ensuring that the joy of watching a live game is not marred by fears for personal safety.

The legacy of the Hillsborough disaster is a profound story of tragedy, resilience, and reform. It serves as a stark reminder of the importance of fan safety, driving continuous improvement in stadium safety standards worldwide. Furthermore, the disaster has fostered a culture of remembrance and learning within football, ensuring that future generations understand the significance of the events of that day and the importance of safeguarding fans. The unyielding pursuit of justice by the victims' families, supported by the football community, underscores the sport's capacity to unite in the face of adversity, advocating for truth and accountability. The Hillsborough disaster, while a moment of profound sadness, has catalyzed changes that have made football a safer space for fans, preserving the integrity of the game and honoring the memory of those who lost their lives.

Nestled in the heart of Liverpool, Anfield isn't just a stadium—it's a temple of dreams, memories, and an undying spirit that transcends generations. This hallowed ground has witnessed some of the most electrifying moments in football, becoming a beacon for fans worldwide. Anfield's allure goes beyond the thrill of matchday; it's a sanctuary where every chant, every cheer, carries the weight of history and the hopes of millions.

This iconic venue stands as a fortress for Liverpool, not merely in terms of the daunting challenge it poses to opponents but as a place of pilgrimage for fans. It's here that the true essence of Liverpool Football Club comes alive, amidst the roar of supporters and the sea of red that fills the stands. The atmosphere is electric, a tangible force that propels the team forward and instills fear in the hearts of those who dare to challenge. Anfield embodies the passion and pride of Liverpool, a place where legends are made and the legacy of the club is celebrated with every game.

The anthem "You'll Never Walk Alone" resonates far beyond the confines of Anfield, serving as a powerful symbol of solidarity and hope. This song, belted out by thousands before each game, wraps the stadium in a cloak of unity, reminding everyone that they are part of something greater. It's a rallying cry, a reassurance in times of adversity, and a celebration in moments of triumph. The anthem transcends football, embodying the spirit of Liverpool as a city and its people's resilience. It connects fans across the globe, creating a sense of belonging and a shared identity that is rare in the world of sports.

Anfield is steeped in rituals and memorials that honor the club's heroes and remember those lost in tragedies like Hillsborough. The Shankly Gates, named after the legendary manager Bill Shankly, stand as a testament to his impact on the club. The Hillsborough memorial, bearing the names of the 97 fans who lost their lives, serves as a poignant reminder of the club's darkest day, ensuring that their memory is forever etched in the heart of Liverpool. These memorials, alongside traditions like the touching of the "This is Anfield" sign before players take to the pitch, connect the present with the past, keeping the club's history alive in the hearts of fans and players alike.

The legacy of Anfield and the ethos of Liverpool Football Club have captivated fans far beyond the city's boundaries, weaving a global tapestry of supporters. The universal appeal of the club's values, embodied in the anthem and the indomitable spirit displayed on the pitch, has drawn fans from all corners of the earth. Social media and fan clubs have played pivotal roles in fostering this worldwide community, creating spaces for fans to share their stories, celebrate victories, and find solace in defeat. This global fanbase stands as a testament to the club's ability to inspire and unite people across different cultures and backgrounds, all under the banner of Liverpool Football Club.

At Anfield, every game is more than just a contest; it's a celebration of football, a tribute to those who have shaped the club's illustrious history, and a demonstration of the unbreakable bond between the team and its supporters. The legacy of this iconic stadium, the traditions it upholds, and the global community it has inspired, underscore the profound impact Liverpool Football Club has had on the world of football and beyond.

39

THE CLASS OF '92: MANCHESTER UNITED'S GOLDEN GENERATION

In the early 1990s, a group of young talents began to make waves in the football world, a set of players who would not only redefine Manchester United but also leave an indelible mark on English football. This ensemble, known as the Class of '92, would transition from promising youth prospects to the core of a team that dominated the domestic and international scene.

The story of the Class of '92 is a tale of growth, from their early days at Manchester United's youth academy to becoming key figures in one of the most successful periods in the club's history. This group, including David Beckham, Paul Scholes, Ryan Giggs, Nicky Butt, Gary Neville, and Phil Neville, showcased the potential of nurturing talent within a club's own system. Their ascent was a blend of individual brilliance and collective effort, underscored by a deep understanding and execution of Sir Alex Ferguson's vision on the pitch. Their transition from youths to legends was marked by an unwavering commitment to excellence, a journey that saw them win numerous Premier League titles, FA Cups, and the iconic

1999 UEFA Champions League, completing a historic treble.

The homegrown nature of the Class of '92 resonated deeply with Manchester United fans, creating a bond that went beyond the usual player-supporter relationship. For fans, these players were a reflection of themselves, embodying the spirit and passion of the local community. This connection was rooted in shared experiences and a mutual understanding of the club's heritage and values. The fans saw in them not just players, but one of their own, individuals who had grown up dreaming the same dreams, walking the same streets, and who now bore the responsibility of carrying forward the club's legacy.

The influence of the Class of '92 extended beyond the confines of Old Trafford, shaping the broader cultural landscape of football. Their success played a pivotal role in highlighting the importance of youth academies, inspiring clubs across England and beyond to invest in developing their own young talents. Furthermore, their journey from the youth ranks to the pinnacle of club football underscored the potential of a well-structured youth system, influencing the approach towards youth development in the sport. Beyond the pitch, their legacy continues at Manchester United, with several members actively involved in football, imparting their knowledge and experiences to the next generation.

The era of the Class of '92 was filled with unforgettable moments that have become part of football folklore. From Beckham's audacious goal from the halfway line against Wimbledon, Scholes' thunderous strikes from outside the box, to Giggs' solo goal in the FA Cup semi-final replay against Arsenal, each member contributed iconic moments that are etched in the memory of fans. These instances were more than just highlights; they were expressions of a team at the zenith of its powers, a group of players who, through sheer talent and determination, turned potential into legendary status. The collective achievements and memorable performances of the Class of '92 not only entertained but also inspired, serving as a beacon for aspiring footballers and a golden chapter in Manchester United's storied history.

In the history of English football, the Class of '92 occupies a special place, a group of players whose journey from youth prospects to legends encapsulates the dreams and aspirations of countless young footballers. Their story is a testament to the power of dedication, a story that underscores the importance of nurturing talent and the profound impact a group of individuals can have on a club and its supporters. The bond they formed with the fans, rooted in shared origins and mutual respect, and their influence on the cultural fabric of the sport, continues to resonate, ensuring that the legacy of the Class of '92 will be celebrated for generations to come.

40

THE GALÁCTICOS: REAL MADRID'S STARS OF THE EARLY 2000S

At the turn of the millennium, Real Madrid embarked on a bold strategy that would forever alter the landscape of football. This approach, famously dubbed the Galácticos policy, was predicated on the notion that assembling a team of superstars would not only guarantee success on the pitch but also catapult the club to unprecedented heights of global fame. The allure of watching Zinedine Zidane, Luis Figo, Ronaldo, and David Beckham share the same dressing room was irresistible, drawing fans from every corner of the globe.

The Galácticos era was marked by an embarrassment of riches in terms of talent. Each signing was a statement, signaling Real Madrid's ambition to not just compete but dominate football's global stage. The arrival of each superstar was an event, celebrated with pomp and fanfare, captivating fans and media alike. This collection of talent under one banner was unprecedented, offering a spectacle that promised brilliance and flair in equal measure.

The anticipation that greeted each new Galáctico was palpable, with fans dreaming of football that was as beautiful as it was victorious. The reality, however, was more nuanced. While there were moments of sheer brilliance and trophies to boot, the expected dominance was often undercut by tactical imbalances and a lack of cohesion. Matches that were supposed to be showcases of superior skill sometimes highlighted the pitfalls of a strategy that prioritized star power over team harmony. Fans were treated to glimpses of the sublime, yet the vision of seamless perfection remained just out of reach.

The Galácticos policy proved to be a masterstroke in terms of marketing and global branding. Real Madrid's appeal skyrocketed, attracting fans who were drawn to the star-studded lineup as much as to the club's rich history. Merchandise sales soared, and the club's games became must-watch events worldwide, establishing Real Madrid as not just a football club but a global brand. This era set new standards for how clubs could leverage player fame to enhance their market position, turning athletes into international icons of the sport.

Looking back, the Galácticos era is remembered for its ambition, its moments of footballing magic, and the lessons it imparted. The strategy underscored the importance of balance within a team, highlighting how a constellation of stars needs a cohesive strategy to truly shine. It also reaffirmed the value of homegrown talent, players who carry the club's ethos in their DNA, complementing the brilliance of imported stars with loyalty and consistency. The legacy of this era is complex, woven with threads of success and cautionary tales, reminding clubs that the heart of football lies in the balance between star power and team unity.

In football history, the Galácticos policy stands out as a bold experiment, a testament to Real Madrid's relentless pursuit of greatness. It was a period that redefined the club's identity, blending ambition with spectacle, and in the process, reshaping the footballing world's perception of what is possible. The stars of the early 2000s may have moved on, but their impact lingers, a chapter in Real Madrid's storied existence that continues to fascinate and instruct.

41

THE SOUND OF SILENCE: PLAYING BEHIND CLOSED DOORS

In the wake of the COVID-19 pandemic, the world of football ventured into uncharted territory. Stadiums, once pulsating with the energy of thousands, stood eerily silent as matches were played behind closed doors. This abrupt shift not only altered the game's physical landscape but also its emotional heartbeat, challenging players and fans to adapt to a reality where the roar of the crowd was replaced by the echo of the ball.

The pandemic's onset saw leagues across the globe grappling with unprecedented challenges. The decision to play matches without fans, though necessary, introduced a stark, surreal aspect to the game. Players found themselves in vast, empty arenas, their shouts and the ball's thud against the net serving as the only soundtrack to the action. This absence of fans, the 12th man, transformed the match atmosphere, affecting dynamics on the pitch in ways previously unimagined. Football, at its core a communal experience, was suddenly devoid of its most vibrant component—the supporters.

Despite the physical barriers imposed by the

pandemic, fans showed remarkable resilience in maintaining a sense of community and support for their teams. Social media platforms and digital forums became the new stadiums, spaces where fans gathered to cheer, lament, and celebrate together. Virtual watch parties mimicked the camaraderie of match days, while fan-generated content kept the spirit alive, showcasing the creativity and passion that fuels football fandom. This period highlighted the adaptability of fans, their ability to find new ways to connect with each other and their teams, underscoring the depth of their commitment.

The silence of empty stadiums had a profound psychological effect on players and the game's ambiance. Athletes, accustomed to drawing energy from the crowd's reactions, had to find new sources of motivation. The lack of immediate feedback, whether cheers for a well-executed play or groans for a missed opportunity, altered players' emotional landscape, potentially impacting decision-making and performance. The absence of fans also shifted the home advantage dynamic, as visiting teams no longer faced the psychological challenge of a hostile crowd. This period provided a stark reminder of the fans' integral role in the emotional and psychological dimensions of football.

This era of pandemic football offered valuable lessons on the irreplaceable role of fans in creating the football experience. The silence underscored the vibrancy fans bring to the game, not just as spectators but as active participants whose energy fuels the passion on the pitch. Clubs and governing bodies recognized the importance of fan engagement, exploring innovative ways to keep fans connected and involved. The pandemic period reaffirmed the essence of football as a shared experience, highlighting the need for inclusivity and engagement strategies that transcend physical boundaries. It was a poignant reminder of football's power to unite, a beacon of hope and community in times of uncertainty.

As football continues to evolve, the lessons from this period of silence and adaptation will resonate, guiding the sport toward a future where the bond between teams and their supporters is stronger and more inclusive than ever. The pandemic underscored the communal soul of football, a testament to the indomitable spirit that defines the beautiful game and its followers.

42

FOOTBALL IN WARZONES: THE POWER OF SPORT

In places where the echoes of conflict drown out the daily lives of its people, football emerges as a beacon of light, offering moments of escape, unity, and sometimes, a catalyst for change. Here, in the shadows of war, the game transforms into something far greater than a sport; it becomes a lifeline.

In regions torn apart by conflict, football serves as a universal language that transcends barriers. Matches organized in the rubble of bombed-out cities provide a semblance of normalcy in an otherwise chaotic existence. One poignant example is seen in makeshift fields in Syria, where amidst the desolation, children and adults alike gather to play, momentarily putting aside the horrors of war. These games, often played with balls made from whatever materials are at hand, symbolize hope and resilience. They remind communities of life before the conflict and offer a vision of what could be once again.

The act of engaging in football in warzones is fraught with dangers. Fields are often located near active conflict zones, putting players and spectators at risk of crossfire or bombings. Additionally, the organization of matches in such areas frequently lacks the security measures found in more stable environments, increasing the potential for harm. Despite these risks, the desire to play and watch the game perseveres, a testament to the sport's powerful draw and its role as a lifeline in times of turmoil.

In certain regions, football has morphed into a symbol of defiance against oppression. Clubs and national teams alike become embodiments of national identity and pride, rallying points for resistance movements. For example, in Palestine, football matches against teams from outside the occupied territories are charged with political significance, serving as platforms to assert national identity and resistance against the Israeli occupation. These matches are more than just games; they are acts of political and social defiance, where every goal scored is a statement of resilience.

The role of football in war-torn communities extends beyond providing a distraction from daily hardships; it plays a significant part in healing and rebuilding the social fabric. The sport offers a space for interaction and communication, breaking down barriers erected by conflict. In Afghanistan, for instance, football leagues have been instrumental in fostering a sense of community and belonging among youth, many of whom have known nothing but war. These leagues not only provide an outlet for physical activity but also serve as a platform for social cohesion, bringing together individuals from diverse backgrounds to share in the collective experience of the game.

In the most unlikely places, under the shadow of conflict and despair, football emerges as a force of unity, hope, and resistance. It proves that even in the harshest conditions, the love for the game endures, offering a glimmer of normalcy and a path toward healing. Through the power of sport, communities find the strength to face another day, to dream of peace, and to envision a future where the sounds of cheering crowds drown out the echoes of war.

43

ONE-ARMED STRIKER: SCORING AGAINST ODDS

One of the most inspiring tales of soccer determination comes from a far-flung corner of Ireland. In the spirited town of Dundalk, where football wasn't just a game but a way of life, the once formidable Dundalk FC was struggling to recapture its former glory. This was the world into which Jimmy Hasty, a one-armed striker from a humble town across the border in Northern Ireland, stepped, destined to leave an indelible mark on the hearts of football fans.

Jimmy wasn't born a football legend. In the rough-and-tumble docklands of Belfast, where he grew up, adversity struck early when he lost his arm in a factory accident at the age of 14. But what he lost in physical capability, he gained in gritty determination. Refusing to let his disability define his limits, Jimmy adapted, honing his skills on the cinder pitches of Sailortown, and soon enough, he was turning heads in local leagues.

When Jim Malone, the charismatic chairman of Dundalk FC, heard about a one-armed wonder scoring goals in Northern Ireland, he was intrigued. Despite skepticism from the board—who saw Jimmy's disability more as a liability—Malone saw something else: unyielding spirit and raw talent. Against the board's initial reservations, he signed Jimmy, betting on his potential to lift the club's fortunes.

Jimmy's debut was the stuff of legends. The town buzzed with curiosity, and the stands at Oriel Park were packed on that chilly November day. Spectators, skeptical and mesmerized in equal measure, watched as the one-armed striker took to the field. What followed was not just a display of skill but a statement. Jimmy scored, weaving through defenders with such grace and precision that it was clear he played by a different set of rules. His performance wasn't just about scoring; it was about leading, inspiring, and defying.

As the seasons unfolded, Jimmy became more than just a player; he became a symbol of defiance against adversity. His ability to dominate in the air, using his body to shield and score, wasn't just effective—it was revolutionary. His stump, often hidden beneath his jersey, became a secret weapon on the pitch, a testament to the idea that limitations only exist if you let them.

His teammates, initially hesitant, soon grew to admire and draw strength from his resilience. On the field, Jimmy was a leader, a creator, orchestrating plays and setting up goals with the vision and finesse of a seasoned maestro. Off the field, he was a friend and a mentor, his life a living lesson in overcoming obstacles.

Under his influence, Dundalk climbed the league tables, their matches becoming must-see events. The crowds swelled, drawn not only by the spectacle but by the man himself. Jimmy turned the club's fortunes around, leading them to a league title in 1963, ending a 30-

year drought and etching his name into the annals of the sport.

But Jimmy's story transcends his on-field exploits. It's about the spirit of a community that rallied behind a man who dared to challenge the norm. It's about a player who, despite losing an arm, gained the admiration and love of a nation. His life off the pitch was as impactful, marked by personal trials, including the tragic end that came too soon, a victim of the sectarian violence that scarred his homeland.

Jimmy Hasty's legacy is more than the sum of his goals or the titles he won. It's captured in the stories still told in Dundalk, in the lives he touched, and in every young player who steps onto a pitch believing in the impossible. His story is a powerful reminder that in football, as in life, it's not the obstacles that define us, but how we overcome them.

44

BRIGHT LIGHTS - YOUNGEST FOOTBALLER IN THE UK

Another great story from Northern Ireland is Christopher Atherton's. Christopher etched his name into the annals of football history when he was still a little boy!

On a seemingly regular League Cup night, Atherton shattered a long-standing record to become the youngest player to ever feature in UK senior football. Entering the game for Glenavon at the tender age of just 13 years and 329 days, he broke the previous record by nearly a year, a record that had stood unchallenged for 42 years since Eamonn Collins made his debut for Blackpool.

Atherton's momentous debut was not just a ceremonial nod in a game already decided; it was a testament to his burgeoning talent and potential. Coming off the bench in the 75th minute against Dollingstown, he immediately made an impact. With his very first touch, Atherton assisted in scoring Glenavon's sixth and final goal of the evening, cementing a 6-0 victory that would be remembered not just for its scoreline but for its historical significance.

This young prodigy's rise is no fluke. His skills have been honed and tested, having trialed at several prominent clubs across the UK, including Dundee United. His performance against Dollingstown wasn't just a glimpse of potential but a demonstration of readiness and composure beyond his years.

The Northern Irish Football Association has been advocating for the inclusion of younger talents in the senior squads as a strategy to elevate the national game's standards. Atherton represents the pinnacle of this initiative, symbolizing the potential benefits of such policies. His debut is a beacon to other clubs, suggesting that youth, when nurtured and trusted, can exceed traditional expectations.

However, replicating this record in leagues like the Premier League or the EFL would be a challenging feat. Stringent regulations in these leagues about the minimum age for players make it unlikely for such young talents to be featured in England's top flights anytime soon. For instance, the Premier League requires players to be at least part of the U16 team, and in the EFL, players must be 15 by September 1 of the playing season to qualify for participation.

Harvey Elliott, who debuted in the Premier League at 16 years and 31 days, currently holds the record in England's highest division, while the EFL has seen even younger talents like Ruben Noble-Lazarus, who played in the Championship at just 15. These players, like Atherton, challenge the norms and inspire a rethinking of what young players can achieve when given a chance.

Christopher Atherton's record-breaking debut isn't just a personal milestone; it's a landmark moment for football in the UK, especially Northern Ireland. It serves as a reminder of the untapped potential residing in young players, urging clubs and governing bodies to reassess how they nurture and integrate budding talents into the highest levels of the sport.

45

THE HEARTBEAT OF PARIS: A TALE OF A FOOTBALLING CITY

In the sprawling suburbs of Paris, where the city's vibrant pulse beats the rhythm of football, a journey begins for many aspiring talents. Ibrahima Traore, a native of Pantin, just outside the northeast corner of Paris, is one such story—a testament to the rich footballing culture that thrives in these neighborhoods.

As Traore stands outside his childhood apartment, overlooking the expansive sports complex where he honed his skills, he reminisces about days spent practicing free-kicks at dawn and dusk. This complex, lovingly referred to as their "Camp Nou" or "Anfield," represents more than just football grounds; it is a crucible where dreams are forged and future stars are born.

Traore's narrative is intertwined with the fabric of Parisian football, where icons like Thierry Henry, N'Golo Kante, and Paul Pogba also emerged. These suburbs, often seen as mere peripheries of the glamorous city center, are actually the heartlands where football pulses strongest. They have produced more talent than any other region in France, a feat highlighted during the 2022 World Cup where thirty players from the vicinity of Paris showcased their skills on the global stage.

This phenomenon can be traced back to the post-war era when immigrants from football-loving nations in North and West Africa settled in these neighborhoods, infusing them with a deep passion for the sport. Local policies further nurtured this passion by ensuring high-quality football facilities were accessible to every child, making the sport a central part of community life.

"You come down from your building, and you have a football field," says Abdelaziz Kaddour, the sports director of FC Montfermeil 93, highlighting the ease with which young talents can access the facilities. This environment has been crucial in developing players like William Saliba and Kylian Mbappe, who found their first footballing steps in these well-equipped local grounds.

The streets of Paris are not just playing fields but classrooms where lessons in dribbling, speed, and tactical awareness are imparted through daily play. The small pitch sizes ensure that players like Sebastien Bassong, who grew up in the northern banlieues, touch the ball frequently, developing a keen sense of the game that larger fields might not afford.

Clairefontaine, the famed academy, stands as a testament to the structured development of these raw talents. Dubbed the "Harvard of football," it is here that players refine their skills, disciplined under a regime that breeds champions. Bassong's journey from the banlieues to Clairefontaine and then onto international fame encapsulates the transformative power of Parisian football education.

However, the path to stardom is crowded with challenges. The sheer abundance of talent has turned the city into a battleground where scouts from top clubs worldwide vie for the next big star. The local leagues, particularly the Ligue de Paris Ile-de-France, are fiercely competitive, boasting over 270,000 players and 1,000 clubs. This competitive environment ensures that only the finest talents rise to the top, hardened by the trials of their youth.

Despite the glamour and success, the Parisian football scene faces criticism for its commercial aspects, particularly at clubs like PSG where homegrown talents often find themselves overshadowed by high-profile international signings. Yet, the grassroots continue to thrive, driven by a community deeply in love with the game.

As the sun sets over Pantin, Traore watches a new generation of players take to the pitches below. The scene is a vibrant tableau of Paris' ongoing football saga—each child with a ball at their feet, a dream in their hearts, and the infinite possibilities of the sprawling cityscape around them.

This journey of Paris as a footballing hotbed is not just about producing athletes; it's about cultivating hope, resilience, and a relentless pursuit of excellence. It's a story that resonates with every young player in Paris, echoing through the banlieues and beyond, a reminder that here, in the heart of France, football is more than a game—it's a way of life.

46

LOSING POINTS OFF THE FIELD: CONTROVERSIAL POINTS DEDUCTION

In the world of football, where every point counts towards glory or survival, point deductions can deliver seismic shocks, reshaping club histories in ways fans and players alike never forget. Here, we delve into some of the most significant point deductions in football history and explore how these penalties have had profound implications on the clubs involved.

Luton Town's Harsh Fall (2008-09 Season)

In the 2008-09 season, Luton Town faced an unprecedented 30-point deduction, one of the harshest penalties ever imposed on a football club. The hefty deduction came as a result of irregular transfer dealings and failing to adhere to administration exit rules. Despite winning the Football League Trophy that same season, the points penalty was a crushing blow, leading to their relegation from the English Football League for the first time in 89 years. This moment marked a dark chapter in the club's history, highlighting how financial mismanagement and regulatory breaches can lead to catastrophic consequences.

Derby County's Double Whammy (2021-22 Season)

Derby County, once a stable Championship side, suffered a 21-point deduction during the 2021-22 season. The club went into administration, triggering an initial 12-point deduction, followed by an additional nine points for financial mismanagement under previous ownership. This massive penalty ultimately confirmed their relegation to League One, despite valiant efforts on the pitch. It was a stark reminder of how financial instability can undermine even the most storied football clubs.

Portsmouth's Financial Downfall (2009-10 Season)

Portsmouth's 2009-10 season was marred by financial chaos, leading to a nine-point deduction after the club went into administration. The penalty all but sealed their fate, resulting in relegation from the Premier League. This scenario underscored the harsh realities of poor financial planning and its direct impact on a club's sporting success, serving as a cautionary tale for other clubs teetering on the edge of financial ruin.

Leeds United's Punishment (2007-08 Season)

Emerging from administration without a proper agreement with creditors, Leeds United faced a 15-point deduction at the start of the 2007-08 season. This penalty hampered their campaign significantly, impacting their promotion ambitions and illustrating the long-term effects of financial distress that had begun to surface years earlier.

Middlesbrough's Controversial Deduction (1996-97 Season)

In one of the most controversial deductions, Middlesbrough was docked three points for failing to fulfill a Premier League fixture against Blackburn in December 1996. The club cited a severe health crisis with a virus affecting the squad, but the league's decision to deduct points ultimately contributed to their relegation by a margin of just two points at season's end. This instance highlighted the potential for point deductions to directly influence competition integrity and the league standings.

The Early Days: Sunderland (1890-91 Season)

Going back over a century, Sunderland was one of the first clubs to suffer a point deduction due to a registration issue with their goalkeeper. The two-point deduction in the 1890-91 season might seem minor compared to modern penalties, but it was significant at the time, impacting their final league position and setting a precedent for strict adherence to league regulations.

Arsenal and Manchester United's Brawl (1990-91 Season)

Turning back the clock, Arsenal and Manchester United were involved in a notorious on-pitch brawl in

1990, which resulted in a two-point deduction for Arsenal and a one-point deduction for United. Despite the deductions, Arsenal still triumphed as league champions, showcasing resilience amidst adversity. This incident not only marked a fierce rivalry but also set a precedent for discipline in the league.

These point deductions across different eras of football reflect a variety of causes, from financial mismanagement and administrative failures to breaches of transfer and registration rules. Each case had significant repercussions for the clubs involved, affecting their league standings, financial health, and in some cases, their very survival in professional football. Clubs like Luton Town and Derby County, in particular, serve as stark reminders of how swiftly fortunes can change in the business of football, with points on the league table sometimes being as volatile as stocks in the market.

For fans, these penalties can be heart-wrenching, transforming seasons of hope into nightmares of relegation battles and financial uncertainty. For the clubs, they are wake-up calls to adhere to fair play, both on and off the pitch. As the stakes continue to rise in the world of professional football, the lessons from these deductions remain ever relevant, serving as cautionary tales for clubs navigating the challenging waters of football finance and governance.

47

THE DAY THE VP STRAPPED ON HIS BOOTS

Picture this: the vice president of your country isn't just running the government, he's also lacing up his soccer boots to run on the field with the national team he owns. Not your typical Tuesday, right? Well, in Suriname, this isn't just a hypothetical—it's a real-life event starring none other than Vice President Ronnie Brunswijk, a man of many talents and just as many controversies.

On a warm and electric evening, 60-year-old Ronnie Brunswijk didn't just oversee his team, Inter Moengotapoe, from the safety of a plush owner's box. No, he marched onto the pitch as a starting striker, proudly wearing the captain's armband at a stadium that bears his name—talk about home field advantage! The crowd was buzzing, the cameras were rolling, and somewhere, the scriptwriters for this seemingly fictional scenario were probably rubbing their hands in glee.

The game kicked off against Olimpia in the CONCACAF League, a match significant enough on its own without the added spectacle of a VP-led team. Brunswijk, moving somewhat less sprightly than his younger counterparts, tried to keep up with the play, his presence alone enough to raise eyebrows and drop jaws around the continent. "Imagine Kamala Harris suiting up for Inter Miami, or Boris Johnson making a dash down the field at Old Trafford," mused one commentator, clearly enjoying the absurdity of the situation.

However, reality kicked in—hard. By the time Ronnie decided to sub himself off 54 minutes into the game, his team was already trailing 3-0. "Now we can say we're 11 vs 11," quipped a commentator, a not-so-subtle nod to the VP's less than professional soccer prowess. Unfortunately for Inter Moengotapoe, Ronnie's departure did little to stem the tide, and the match ended in a 6-0 thumping.

Post-match, the scene shifted from surreal to slightly bizarre, as footage emerged of Brunswijk waltzing into the opposition's locker room and handing out wads of cash to the Olimpia players. Whether it was a gesture of good sportsmanship or something more eyebrow-raising, it only added another layer to the legend of the day the VP played.

Ronnie Brunswijk isn't your run-of-the-mill politician. His resume reads like a blockbuster action film: elite paratrooper, rebel leader, soccer player, and somehow, amidst battling military dictatorships and trafficking accusations, he also found time to father at least 50 children. In 2005, he was suspended from Suriname's national football association after a notably heated moment involving a handgun and a player on the pitch.

In a world where politicians often stick to their podiums, Ronnie Brunswijk reminds us that sometimes, they also strap on their boots, whether we think they should or not. And in doing so, he turned an ordinary Tuesday into a day that the football world—and surely the citizens of Suriname—won't soon forget.

48

A TALE OF PATIENCE: 19 YEARS BETWEEN TWO GAMES

In the heart of Milan, where the colors blue and black adorn the dreams of young footballers, the story of Alex Cordaz stands out—a tale of unwavering persistence, extensive journeys across football landscapes, and an inspiring return to where it all began.

Alex Cordaz, a bright prospect from Inter Milan's youth academy, first donned the prestigious Nerazzurri colors as a U20 player, signaling the start of what many hoped would be a fruitful career at the top of Italian football. His raw talent and dedication led to a momentous day on February 4, 2004, when he made his debut in a thrilling Coppa Italia draw against Juventus. For a young goalkeeper, playing against such illustrious opposition was nothing short of a dream come true.

However, the path to football stardom is seldom straight. Despite his initial breakthrough, Cordaz found himself as the third-choice goalkeeper, a position that promised more bench time than play. His journey would soon take him far from the San Siro, on a winding road through Italy and beyond.

From 2004 to 2005, Cordaz was loaned out to Spezia and then to Acireale, gathering experience in Italy's lower leagues. His journey took a more permanent turn in 2006 when he signed joint-ownership deals first with Treviso, then with Pizzighettone. Each stint offered him precious game time, though neither culminated in a lasting stay, especially after Treviso disbanded due to financial difficulties.

Seeking stability and new challenges, Cordaz ventured to Switzerland in 2009, joining FC Lugano. Over two seasons, he became a mainstay in the team, making 56 appearances that showcased his growth and reliability as a goalkeeper. The Italian's journey didn't stop there; he returned to Italy to play for Citadella in Serie B, where over two seasons, he made 80 appearances, replacing his former Inter teammate, Simone Villanova.

His travels continued as he moved to Parma in 2013, and although loaned to Slovenian side ND Gorica, he managed to impress with 35 appearances. The following years saw him loaned to Crotone, where after a season, his consistent performances led to a full contract.

As seasons changed and years turned, the memory of wearing the black and blue of Inter Milan—a brief episode in the early days of his career—remained vivid in Cordaz's mind. In an unexpected twist of fate, nearly two decades after his debut, Inter Milan called again. In July 2021, at the age of 38, Alex Cordaz made a nostalgic return to Inter Milan.

It wasn't until 2023, a staggering 19 years after his first appearance, that Cordaz would step onto the pitch for Inter Milan once again. This second game was not just a testament to his skill and determination but a symbolic homecoming to the place where his professional journey began.

Alex Cordaz's career is a narrative of perseverance. In a sport where youth and peak physical fitness are prized, Cordaz defied the norms, maintaining his standards through rigorous discipline and an undying love for football. His journey speaks volumes about the mental fortitude required to stay at one's best, even when the path leads away from the limelight into quieter, distant stretches of a footballer's road.

For young players at Inter Milan's academy, Cordaz's story is a beacon of hope and a lesson in resilience. It tells them that the journey might take them far and wide, through unexpected turns and seemingly endless waits, but with determination, the road can lead back to dreams long cherished.

In the end, Alex Cordaz didn't just return to Inter Milan; he returned as a seasoned veteran, a man shaped by his experiences, ready to inspire the next generation with his enduring commitment to the beautiful game. His tale, rich in its trials and triumphs, remains a profound chapter in the annals of Inter Milan, celebrated not just for the games played, but for the spirit of never giving up.

49

THE MOST BRUTAL GAME IN HISTORY

In the football history books, few games have ever encapsulated the raw intensity and unyielding ferocity of the 1970 FA Cup Final Replay between Leeds United and Chelsea. Played under the floodlights of Old Trafford, this match not only defined an era but left a big mark on the storied histories of both clubs.

Leeds United, known for their hard-nosed approach and tactical discipline under manager Don Revie, were seen as the strong, gritty representatives of the North. Chelsea, on the other hand, embodied the flamboyant, carefree spirit of London's King's Road, mixing celebrity with a dash of footballing flash. Their contrasts couldn't have been starker, and their similarities more provocative, setting the stage for a clash that was about more than just a trophy—it was a battle for identity and pride.

From the initial whistle, the match lived up to its billing as a bruising encounter. Eddie Gray, Leeds' skillful winger, quickly became a target for Chelsea's defenders, notably David Webb, who had suffered at Gray's hands in their previous meeting. Within minutes, the tackles flew in, hard and fast, with Webb delivering a particularly harsh welcome back to Gray that set the tone for the evening.

As the game wore on, the physicality escalated. Norman Hunter, Leeds' uncompromising defender known for his tough tackling, was met with boos and jeers from Chelsea fans every time he touched the ball. His duels in the midfield often ended with players from both sides on the ground, nursing bruises or worse. Chelsea's Ron "Chopper" Harris lived up to his nickname, taking special interest in ensuring Leeds' wingers knew he was there.

Referee Eric Jennings, overseeing what would be his final match before retirement, seemed reluctant to clamp down on the game's excessive physicality. His leniency allowed the game to flow but also to boil over. Hugh McIlvanney of The Observer later noted that Jennings seemed to require a death certificate before awarding a free-kick, highlighting the game's notorious nature.

Amid the chaos, there were moments of sheer brilliance. Chelsea's goalkeeper, Peter Bonetti, despite suffering a painful knee injury, pulled off save after save, keeping Chelsea in the game with heroic defiance. Leeds' attacks, orchestrated by the brilliant but battered Billy Bremner, were relentless but ultimately fruitless, stymied by Chelsea's resolute defense and Bonetti's acrobatics.

The game reached its zenith in extra time. A long throw by Ian Hutchinson, flicked on by Jack Charlton, found its way to Webb, who headed home the decisive goal. The goal not only secured Chelsea's first FA Cup win but also a revenge sweetened by the bitterness of their previous encounters with Leeds.

The 1970 FA Cup Final Replay remains one of the most talked-about matches in the history of English football, remembered as much for its ferocity as for its football. Refereed twice more in hindsight, the game would have seen multiple red cards in today's game, a testament to its brutal nature.

Years later, the rivalry has cooled, the players have aged, and football has evolved. Yet, the match is still recalled with a mix of awe and horror, a brutal ballet that showcased the best and worst of football in that era. It remains a touchstone for discussions about sportsmanship, rivalry, and the changing norms of football—a game that was, perhaps, the most brutal ever played.

50

THE LITTLE GIANTS: SAN MARINO'S JOURNEY OF HOPE AND HEART

In the heart of Europe, nestled in the embrace of Italy, lies the serene and scenic microstate of San Marino. Known for its stunning mountaintop views and medieval architecture, San Marino also carries a unique distinction in the world of soccer. It's home to the national team often dubbed as the world's most persevering underdog.

Matteo Vitaioli, San Marino's most capped player, embodies the spirit of his team. A graphic designer by day and a footballer by heart, Vitaioli's dedication to his nation's team is unwavering, despite the challenging odds they face every match. It has been 17 years since Vitaioli first donned the sky blue jersey of San Marino, and in those years, victory has been an elusive companion.

The country's sole win still resonates through the streets of San Marino—a 1-0 triumph over Liechtenstein back in April 2004, which remains a beacon of hope and a reminder of what passion and perseverance can achieve. Andy Selva, the nation's all-time leading scorer, sealed the win with an early goal that has become a legendary tale for every Sanmarinese.

Despite the scarcity of victories, every match for San Marino is a display of immense national pride and collective effort. Vitaioli recalls the difficult moments with a philosophical air, particularly the grueling 11-0 defeat against the Netherlands in 2011. Such experiences, though painful, have forged a bond among the players that transcends the sport.

San Marino's squad, composed largely of amateurs who balance day jobs with their footballing duties, is a testament to their love for the game. Each match, regardless of the score, is played with a hope and a tenacity that is rarely seen in the professional realm. Vitaioli, now a father and a seasoned player, still treasures the dream of playing a pivotal role in earning his team's second official win.

Recent matches have shown promising sparks of improvement. Scoring in consecutive games for the first time in 18 years has ignited a renewed sense of self-belief among the players. Filippo Berardi, another of San Marino's committed warriors, recently made headlines by scoring a crucial penalty against Finland, marking a historic moment for the team by scoring in three consecutive matches.

Berardi's enthusiasm encapsulates the team's new ethos. Despite the historical defeats, the joy derived from scoring a goal, even when the outcome of the game is already decided, is immense. Each goal scored by San Marino is celebrated like a victory, each game played is a step forward.

As San Marino prepares for upcoming matches, the sense of anticipation is palpable both on and off the pitch.

The national team, under the guidance of their new coach Roberto Cevoli, harbors ambitions not just to compete, but to conquer and create moments of joy for their supporters.

Cevoli, a local who has spent his entire footballing career in San Marino, is optimistic about transforming the team's fortunes. "I want to dream with no limits," he declares, encapsulating the undying spirit of San Marino. With each training session, each strategy meeting, and each friendly game, Cevoli and his team are slowly but surely laying the groundwork for what could be another historic win.

In San Marino, football is more than just a game; it's a celebration of national pride, a display of unyielding spirit against all odds. The players are not just athletes; they are heroes who carry the hopes of their nation every time they step onto the field.

As the sun sets over the ancient towers of San Marino, the lights in the small stadium flicker on, ready for another evening of training. The players gather, a band of brothers, ready to sweat and strive not just for victory, but for the honor of representing the Most Serene Republic of San Marino.

Win or lose, San Marino's story is one of inspiration, a tale that reminds us that sometimes, the heart and spirit of the game are just as important as the scoreline.

CONCLUSION

Hey there,

What a ride, huh? We've zigzagged through the lush fields of grassroots football, ducked into the electrifying stadiums hosting World Cup finals, and mingled with fans whose hearts beat in sync with the pulse of the game. Football, this universal language, has once again shown its power to bridge continents, merge cultures, and stitch together a patchwork of beliefs and backgrounds in a shared, undying passion for the game.

From the underdog tales that had us on the edge of our seats to the strategic masterminds revolutionizing tactics on the pitch, we've explored the vast, vibrant world of football. The stories of Lionel Messi's journey from Rosario to Barcelona, and Leicester City's fairy-tale Premier League win, weren't just tales. They were powerful sermons on determination, resilience, and the relentless pursuit of dreams.

And let's not forget the lessons learned along the way. We dived into the evolution of football tactics, the pivotal role of youth academies, and the game-changing impact of technology in modern football. Each chapter wasn't just a story; it was a classroom, enriching your understanding of the beautiful game.

The soul of football, though, is its fans. From Dortmund's Yellow Wall to the echoing chants of "You'll Never Walk Alone" at Anfield, it's clear: football is nothing without its fans. Their passion, their energy, it's the lifeblood of this sport, fueling the magical atmosphere that makes football what it is.

Now, I want to turn the spotlight to you. Dream big. Pursue your passions with the same fire and spirit that the heroes of our tales showed. And while you're at it, share your own football story. Whether you've graced the pitch, cheered till your voice cracked, or simply dreamed of doing so, your story matters. How has football touched your life? How has it inspired you?

I'm genuinely thankful you joined me on this journey. Your companionship has been as thrilling as a last-minute winner. I hope these tales have ignited a spark within you, as they have in me. Let's not end the conversation here. Hit me up on social media. Share your thoughts, your favorite football moments, or how the game has inspired you.

Looking ahead, the future of football is as bright as a floodlit stadium on a Champions League night. The game will continue to evolve, enchant, and inspire, weaving new stories for generations to come. The tales in this book? They're just the beginning. Football's legacy is eternal, its power to inspire, boundless.

Here's to the beautiful game and its endless possibilities.

Cheers, Sam

www.ingramcontent.com/pod-product-compliance
Lightning Source LLC
Chambersburg PA
CBHW072200070526
44585CB00015B/1230